D1172993

SECURE FROM CRIME

How To Be Your Own Bodyguard

2nd Editon

Completely revised, improved and expanded

by

Craig Fox Huber
and
Don Paul

About the authors: Craig Fox Huber is a former Marine, a weapons specialist, and a feature writer for various outdoor magazines. He spends much of his working time as one of the top executive protection specialists in the world. Don Paul, a law school graduate, is a former Green Beret and police officer. He's the author of several outdoor survival books.

> " I don't advocate disregard for the law, but sometimes one's own life takes precedence over regard for the fine points of modern law." *Craig Huber*
> "Don't worry about being right; be righteous. Fight crime: shoot back. Crime has increased over 560% since the early sixties. Shouldn't we change our game plan?" *Don Paul*

Cover: Alan Iglesias of Escondido

Gratitude: To the manufacturers of home and personal defense devices. These people produce products and devices which help preserve your life and freedom. Each one you purchase lessens your chances of becoming a victim.

A.M.D.G.

Prayer: Before we publish, we bow our heads. *Lord, we want to rededicate our hearts to you as this book comes alive. Our lives are yours, our works are yours, and we acknowledge your Holy Scripture as standing forever. We believe our world is filled with crime because we've departed from your principles. We worship you, Father, and give you all the glory. Amen.*

Library of Congress Catalog Card Number: 92-81773

Publisher's Cataloging in Publication

Huber, Craig F., 1943- & Paul, Don, 1937-
        Secure from crime: How to be your own bodyguard / by Craig Fox Huber and Don Paul
        p. cm.
        Includes index
        ISBN 0-938263-18-8
        1. Crime Prevention. 2. Self Defense. 3. Self Defense for women. I. Paul, Don, 1937- II. Title
        HV7431.H83 1993   362.88
                                                                  QBI92-2012

INTRODUCING. . .
QUICK READER BOOKS by PATH FINDER
New-method, how-to books.

To take a productive place in society, a writer has to focus on one goal. In this book, our goal is: **To protect your life.** That's what a bodyguard does for a client. Your bodyguard isn't just any bodyguard, either. He earns about a thousand a day guarding some of the richest royalty in the world, not only in the U.S., but while travelling all over the globe.

At Path Finder, we have a different publishing philosophy. We take our best shot at going <u>beyond any other knowledge in a given field.</u> In this book, for example, we had to interview some of the worst offenders to learn the nuts and bolts of street crime. Then we developed counter-tactics. In swift, easy-to-understand detail, you can read about the newest crimes and our way of defending against them.

Though this information is life-saving and critical, the text is written and specially formatted for speed reading. Maybe it's choppy, but <u>we think you'll get it---fast.</u> Our electronic scrubbers report:

> At the sub-vocalization reading rate of less than 600 wpm, you should complete this whole book in 1 hour, 29 minutes, not including box additions, which we provide for concentration relief. After scrubbing, we achieved reading-ease parity with Hemingway's short stories. We average under 1.4 syllables per word. Our average sentence: Under 15 words. We cut graphic description paragraphs by more than half with our illustrations.

Path Finder began over 10 years ago. We first invented a way to keep you from getting lost in the woods without using a map; it was called, _Never Get lost. The Green Beret's Compass Course,_ Over 25,000 copies are in print. After that, we added to our book list and widened our distribution. We published:

Everybody's Outdoor Survival Guide
Great Livin' in Grubby Times best selling survival book.
Everybody's Knife Bible over 30,000 copies!
24 + Ways to Use Your Hammock in the Field.
How to Write a Book in 53 Days. We teach our audience how to write as fast and efficiently as this book can be read.

A

We develop and write about new ideas and methods. We're the innovative people who wrote about outdoor know-how and discovered:

√A two-ounce, 30¢ wilderness bed for sleeping above ground.

√The light for your hunting knife sheath so the ground is illuminated for you in the jungle or woods at night.

√Paint for the bottom of your outdoor boots to make them slippery. Wear the paint off the bottom; they no longer clog with mud.

√How to use animals to double your survive-ability.

√Green Beret team concepts applied to survival groups so you can enjoy the ultimate life-style outdoors.

All our books have gone into multiple editions. Most major outdoor magazines have reviewed our books and our systems have been adopted by many outdoor organizations. We publish only in paperback. <u>Once you own any of our books, you can order a new, updated copy for half price, no questions asked.</u>

(See the order coupon in the back of this book.)

One more thing---

Note also, the boxes like this at the end of each chapter contain recreational reading---polemics and provoking thoughts on crime. **No political forum is intended.**

We wrote this because: More than any constitutional right a criminal has, you have a right to live your life in peace---free of danger. <u>We're sure that many of our readers will save both property and lives as a result of owning this book.</u> Many will escape being a victim because of what you learned here; feel free to write to us with your own story.

How to stay. . .
SECURE FROM CRIME
How To Be Your Own Bodyguard
Table of Contents

Foreword. Path Finder, providers of easy-to-understand information, hires an internationally experienced executive protection specialist and a former Green Beret **to save your life.** They teach you how to live crime-free and stay alive.

b

SECURE FROM CRIME

How To Be Your Own Bodyguard
by
Craig Fox Huber
and
Don Paul

INTRODUCTION

After this book was first published, the authors appeared on over 90 radio shows within 6 months and asked this question: **"Would you like to be eligible for police assistance?"** If you were one of the listeners, did you answer, "yes?" Well, here's some news: Police can only make an arrest <u>after</u> a crime has been committed. Translation: To be eligible for police assistance, you have to pre-qualify---by becoming a victim. Knowing that, how would you answer? If you want the police to assist you, wait until a crime occurs. You won't have long; we guarantee. But if you don't want to be victimized, learn how to avoid crime <u>before</u> it happens, or how to defeat it <u>during</u> its occurrence. Otherwise, call the cops and give them your report---if you can . . . Here's the crime defense motto:

"Fail to prepare, and you prepare to fail."

"Be prepared." For what? Violent crime; that's what. Our world just isn't a safe place anymore. Therefore, **to survive in this society, you either have to hire a full time bodyguard, or learn to be your own.**

1

In former times, our criminal justice system protected citizens. Law breakers paid severe penalties. House burglars knew they might get shot. Murderers were caught, convicted and executed. The safest place to live today is on death row---where in 1993, far less than a hundred people died. On city streets, however, over 10,500 people were killed tragically. According to one Federal report, violent crime killed more people than AIDS. What are criminals doing to America, and what should our attitude be? G. Gordon Liddy stated the case when *Forbes Magazine* published his article, "Security."

"There are essentially two kinds of people in this world, and they can be distinguished easily by their reaction to life-threatening situations such as the invasion of one's home. All resort to prayer. But it is by the text of their prayers ye shall know them. For some it's a version of `God, please don't let them find me,' then when found, `God, please don't let them hurt me.' Sometimes the plea is for a miracle: `God, please let the police get here in time!' Such persons have elected to be life's victims and, indeed, only God can help them.

There are others, however, who've chosen not to be victims, and to whom it has occurred that God may, from time to time, be busy on another line and it might be prudent to do the necessary thing to protect themselves. Their prayer, left on the divine answering machine, is for the intruder: `May God have mercy on your soul.' This article is for them."

You'll begin to understand crime and its effect on our society when you look at it as a disease. **Consider criminals as germs and viruses.** Our courts and penal system limit the cure, so the disease spreads and flourishes. If doctors worked under the same restraints as police do today, they couldn't practice medicine; germs and viruses would have rights! No health official could kill mosquitoes until *after* they had bitten and infected you. You couldn't take penicillin until *after* an infection had done irreparable damage. Even with infections roaring in your body, only limited amounts of cure could be applied.

Today, the "germs" have the upper hand. The police can do little until *after* a crime has been committed. Even if a criminal *is* caught and sent to prison (for curing), our system seems to pamper him. What **is** jail, anyway? It's a place where criminal germs meet and breed, get shelter, a bed, and three meals a day, all at your expense. Jail is a punishment only if you don't have anything in common with the people who are already there.

Crime is on the upswing everywhere. You'd better develop a personal defense plan for yourself and your home immediately. Take some simple and basic precautions; otherwise, plan on becoming a victim. Get ready now; later, when some germ attacks or invades, will be too late. If you want to *win during* the inevitable battle, you'll have to prepare *now*.

To develop a correct mind set about crime and how it relates to you, listen to Mayor Pratt Kelley from Washington, D.C. "We've got a war on our hands," she said during a news conference in Oct 93. She appealed to President Clinton for National Guard help. But while Washington, D.C. is bad, no major city in the U.S. is at peace.

Why? Because politicians really don't mean "war" in the military sense. Otherwise, crime would be decreasing. In a real war, for example, you don't capture the enemy and then turn them loose with an early release program so they can shoot at you again. You don't give aid and comfort to the enemy. But that's what's happening, and only you can defend yourself and your family.

If you want to survive, start by knowing this: Somebody out there wants to attack you or your family. Your property, your body, or your life mean nothing to these people. The criminal's rebellion against the law makes him a hero. Fueled by a deep-seated resentment and bitterness, the compulsion to rob and kill controls him.

He already hates you. Understand this: It appears to be a personal problem he has with you, but it isn't.   He hates, period. If you're not in his or her family or gang, hatred rages, and <u>you are the target</u>. Witness the violent deaths in the news. Other victims, hundreds of them, didn't appear in the news because they didn't die. Even so, they were robbed, raped, or crippled. For how much? Oftentimes, for a few bucks. Like a car burglar who causes hundreds of dollars in vehicle damage to rip off a $25 CB radio, the amount they steal isn't important. But stealing inflates his image, so he's always looking for new victims. Those victims never had a chance to decide whether they wanted to be at war.   Neither do you.

In order to survive this war, take advice from those who's job it is, and has been, to keep others safe. Craig Huber was a Marine and is now a top personal security consultant. Don Paul was a Green Beret and has written several successful books on outdoor survival. He worked for years as a police officer. Both know:
<u>The best way to win a war is to know your enemy,</u>
<u>and make your battle plans accordingly</u>.

What are gangs producing? Why does crime exist? Where does all the violence come from?   Lack of self esteem, which causes a compulsion to raise themselves above others. The need for self esteem demands that A. they make something of themselves, B. that they acquire things so *it looks like* they've made something of themselves, or C. that they win in sports, at work, or in other achievements so *they can say* they made something out of themselves. Different sub-cultures put different values on achievement. For many it's how much money they earn. To a criminal germ, it's how big the score is on the goods he steals. Expressed by a gang member in October 1992 on the Jerry Springer television talk show, "You got to earn your respect." Many gang members believe the greatest honor they can earn is to die for their gang's colors. (We would like to see them all so honored.)

4

Edward James Olmos, star of *Miami Vice* and the feature film, *American Me*, said, "The newest craze isn't gang violence; it's random violence . . ." The random violence comes from a mal-adjusted psychopath who thinks of himself as a nobody and is looking for an upper-type, equalizing thrill. Thus the killing. Hardened criminals think it's a real rush to break into a house, steal a car, snatch a purse, or kill somebody. Succeed, and peers consider them a hero. Most gangs promote members according to how much violence they commit.

This is the new street ethic: "Whatever you're not strong enough to keep belongs to me." Is there an effective deterrent for today's criminal? Yes---fear of pain, injury, or death. These are deterrents you'll have to supply when faced with a crime. Going to prison is no big deal; for a gang member, it's like old home week.

Given attitudes sparked by hatred and the low self image welfare gives the taker, how does most crime take place? Almost by accident. Right now, as you read this, thousands of criminals, straight out of prison on early release, are roving about, seeking out, a victim. You, or your property become somebody's prey because you collide by accident. You, the victim, got in a criminal's way. The germs and attackers were committed to the act long before they picked you to be the victim. In a gang members own words: "Hey, I'm just out there to get what's mine."

Where do we face threats? Everywhere! We're at risk anytime we are exposed to the public. Today, in any major U.S. city, we're in danger of being caught in the middle of violence. Perhaps you can apply the great bodyguard maxim. **"Don't get out of trouble. Keep out of trouble."**

That's why we wrote this book. Cops become involved **after** you become a victim. While you bleed in the back of an ambulance, they write up the reports and start looking for the attacker. This book shows you how to take care of the problem **beforehand.** We'll reduce your chances of being attacked or robbed and enable you to do what most good soldiers are trained to do—-minimize risk and carry on with life's mission.

Even while minimizing your chances of becoming a victim, you still may find yourself in a battle. Because it might happen, we'll show you how to **defeat the enemy---**decisively! Caution: Some of the methods in this book are illegal in some states. We don't advocate disrespect for the law, but authors have a duty to tell the whole truth, so we wrote about how some people get around the law to protect themselves. See, *AFTER THE ATTACK.*

GENERAL DEFENSE PLAN AGAINST CRIME
In the movie, *The Untouchables,* Sean Connery (1930's Irish street cop) twice asks Kevin Costner (as Elliot Ness, FBI agent enforcing prohibition), **"What are you prepared to do?"** The first time was during a conversation on the street. The second time, Connery was on the floor of his home in a pool of blood, and it was his last question. We're asking you the same question now. Can you develop a toughened mind-set? Knowing how the enemy thinks will help you develop an attitude against being a victim. Sometimes our own attitudes are a bit harsh. But we think yours would be the same if you talked to the victims and listened to the criminals in the streets.

We want you to live in much improved safety and peace. Many people have called in and cried out during the radio shows we've done. Others have asked about paranoia.

We don't want you to be scared---just conduct your life as if you are. Turn up your perception knob; learn to be your own bodyguard.

6

Chapter 1

PERSONAL DEFENSE MEASURES

Study the job of a bodyguard and you'll learn: dead clients don't write checks. If you don't protect your client, you don't get paid---and you shouldn't. What's the best way to succeed at your job? Anticipate and plan, or *planticipate*. Look for trouble, then avoid it. Anytime you have to pull your weapon, smack an intruder or drive like a New York cabbie to get away from trouble, you probably failed to plan properly or just plain screwed up.

Today, many areas of the United States are much like Vietnam during the war. We own it during the day, but the night belongs to criminals. Many neighborhoods are no longer safe. You would be amazed at the number of attacks on "ordinary, honest citizens" which occur in places you'd think a sensible person would avoid. I'm sure those victims who survived wish they had planned or done things differently.

You can learn from their mistakes. For example, instead of visiting a convenience store after 11:00 PM, do without a gallon of milk or a candy bar. The incidents of rape and assault near convenience stores, especially those within easy walking distance of college dorms, is extremely high. If you need something after hours, try to find a store frequented by the local police on their coffee breaks. Feel free to introduce yourself. If they know you and consider you a "friend," they are more likely to respond to your call for help. Also, in a violent confrontation on your property, probably at night, they're less likely to confuse you with a perp (perpetrator, one who commits a crime).

The 24 hour Auto-Tellers are just too dangerous to use after dark. It's easy for a perpetrator with a gun to persuade you to rob your own bank account on his behalf. Avoid these areas of high risk if at all possible. If you simply must get cash, remember, there's safety in numbers. Wait in your car until more customers are there. Lock your car! If you have taken firearms training and you practice regularly, carry a weapon! Don't think that after you've completed your transaction, you're safe, either. Some perps will wait in the shadows and ambush you as you return. They wait for you in the dark or hide---either behind, under, or even in---your car. At least, carry a five-cell flashlight. Shine the light slowly into every dark corner or shrub around you. Bounce the light off adjacent walls and check the shadows. A tree outline with a standing bump behind it means trouble. Incidentally, these flashlights also work well as a club.

Other areas are dangerous, too. Be particularly cautious in all parking lots, community parks, construction sites, and amusement parks. Avoid carnivals, poorly lit streets, pawn shop and X-rated movie areas, red light districts, hangouts for drug peddlers and users, areas with a vagrant populace (like beach parking lots), and areas with a high concentration of derelict buildings. Any one of these places could well be the last place you visit.

Hospitals are now hazardous to your health in one specific area—parking lots. Weirdoes just love the target-rich environment offered by shift-changing nurses. The thugs 'n drugs crowd like to pick on doctors and their vehicles. Visit hospitals during the early afternoon hours whenever possible. Ask security to escort you to your car. If you go alone (in the dark especially) your left hand opens the door while your right hand stays in your purse or pocket on spray gas or a handgun. Don't nose into parking spaces; back in. You may need to get away quickly. Scan the side (door) windows of your car as you get in. Look for a reflection of movement.

WATCH OUT IN ELEVATORS

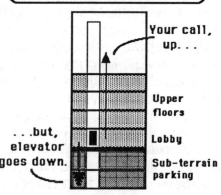

ELEVATORS PROGRAMMED TO ASSIST CRIMINALS IN THE BASEMENTS

Your call, up...

Upper floors

...but, elevator goes down.

Lobby

Sub-terrain parking

ELEVATORS ARE: Small cells travelling up or down in which no help is available. Take stairs.

Your health will benefit from your climbing stairs. So will your safety. Older public elevators are dangerous. If you step into one from the lobby and select an upper floor, it may still go down to answer the call of the thief or pervert lurking in the basement or underground parking. When you arrive there alone, they get you. Solution: Step in by yourself from the lobby. Push, B and 5 (Basement and any upper floor), then step back out into the lobby. Now, while standing in the lobby, push the call button to go up. On the elevator location indicator on top of the main doors, watch it go down to the basement and return. When it stops at the lobby empty, climb aboard to go up safely. Even though the thug in the basement keeps pushing the call button, your elevator knows it was just there and won't answer his call until you are safely delivered.

If your elevator stops before you get where you're going and a suspicious thug gets in, step off. Failing that, stand near the operating panel in case you need help. The red stop button sounds an immediate alarm.

WOMEN ALONE

Just as a fish goes for a lure in water, your purse attracts a druggie coming down off a crack high. Purse snatching isn't particularly profitable, but it's popular because it's easy and fast. It doesn't take much of a brain to grab a purse and run. Think about the psychological state of the perpetrator. Many street robbers are just coming down off their latest drug binge. To say the least, it makes them moody. They don't have time to figure out a complicated crime. They need—now, and women's purses are everywhere, so they grab and go.

Subway perps often stand near their victim and grab the purse just before the doors close. The perp walks free as the robbed victim moves down the track behind closed doors. Recently, two thugs in Los Angeles drove along close to the sidewalk and grabbed a purse belonging to a 94-year-old woman. They dragged her over a hundred feet to a horrible death before getting away. On the street and in supermarket parking lots, purse snatching from a vehicle happens all the time; that's why we teach you to walk against traffic. In parking lots, walk up the driving isles against the arrows. That way, all cars drive towards you. Some germ can't hang out a car window and grab from behind. Remember, if someone does take your purse, they often get your home keys and identification with your street address on it. Change your locks! If they get your purse with ID and keys, they'll pick you clean at your home address without having to break in.

Hide your purse! Attach a long carrying strap to your purse and carry it over your shoulder, under your coat. If you're carrying something valuable, and it looks as if you're being stalked, you can ditch your purse in any mail box and get it back from the post office later. Also, know that expensive purses appear to carry more loot inside. Buy a nylon belt purse (also called a fanny pack) and buckle it around your waist. If you don't feel comfortable without a purse, spread most of your money and credit cards around. Inside shirt and coat pockets make good stash places. So do the tops of socks or stockings.

THE LATEST ON PURSE SNATCHING

Someone snatches your purse with your ID, house keys, business keys, and business cards, etc. A few days later, you get a call: In a sweet voice, "Ms Jones, I found your purse in a trash bin with everything in it. If you would like, I could meet you at a restaurant. Oh, would you please bring me a small reward? I'll wait right here, but I only have a little time."

You can go, but **don't leave your house unguarded.** Scam: They watch you leave; your address was in your purse. Then, with the keys they enter and clean out your house! Counter scam: Leave quickly, but call a friend to come and scope your house out with binoculars and cellular. She can call police during the burglary; probably, the burglars have your purse!

Statistics show, you're especially vulnerable just as you step onto the street or parking lot. Don't get out of your car without scanning your mirrors and taking a good look around. Husbands, be your wife's LIFO, (Last In, First Out). She gets into the car first to drive while you scan the perimeter. When you arrive, check first for potential dangers before you get out of the car to make sure her safe exit is secure.

Women, especially alone: You are a prime target for robbery and assault. You're perceived to be weaker, and supposed to be easier to scare. Besides, the perp worries less about getting hurt. Recently, we noticed some appalling situations.

Scene: Supermarket. Mom leaves shopping cart with small child and purse in it to go a couple isles over and study grocery labels.

Scene: Parking lot. A mother left her children in the car with windows rolled down, engine running (air condition on) and keys in ignition.

No matter where you are, you'll have to become more security conscious. The following may seem impractical or extreme, but lock your doors all the time. Don't make unnecessary trips anywhere---especially into major cities without a companion. Stay behind privacy curtains at home, and tinted windows in your car. Finally, watch your telephone security. Give out no information; talk to no strangers; list no phone numbers; and, don't allow strangers into your space. If your car breaks down, **do not** accept help from a stranger. Let him know you **do not** want help before he gets out of his car. The slightest social contact with some men who stop to help a lady can be trouble. Once your car is fixed, they think you owe them. Ask a helpful stranger to notify police; nothing more.

ARMED MUGGING---THE MORE PERSONAL TOUCH

Consider the psychological state of the mugger. He may be just dropping down off a drug high. You think you had a bad day? This is the worst. So, he pulls a knife and says, "Give me your wallet!" **Do not argue!** The attitude you'll encounter is sub-human, maybe drug-driven. Stay safe! Nothing you own is worth a stab wound injury.

Don't respond aggressively; don't threaten or warn. That makes perps horribly mad. The idea is not to die. Instead, buy life by cooperating as best you can. Be gracious and say something like: "No problem, take it all." Wait for your chance to escape. Insure your life with whatever you can give him. Make sure you have something to give too—at least $10, better $20. Even with a young teenager, bargaining or arguing can be dangerous. Often, this may be his first armed robbery; if you "*dis" him, you "dis" his set (gang origination) and he'll <u>have to</u> kill you. More than anything, a gangbanger wants love and acceptance he couldn't get from a family. Therefore, he is "down for the set" which means he is willing to die (or kill you) for it.

*(Dis. Short for disrespect, the word is so commonly used on the street it now appears in a special version of the Bible.)

CREDIT CARD=DEATH WARRANT IN A MUGGING

Don't carry credit cards with your money. If your credit card is in your wallet or purse, you may get shot. Fences pay higher prices for stolen cards when they know the victim is dead and therefore can't cancel the card right away.

This is a most serious problem. ATM rip-offs cost Americans 18 million a year. Credit card fraud costs 3.5 billion! Last year, we suffered a 22% increase. Source: Gary Tomlinson, American Security Research.

Solution: Credit card companies need to issue a personal code number or a phony name (like a CB handle) that only the customer can use while charging. Thus, anyone else signing the customer name would risk getting caught when they tried to use the card. Also, since few perps have loyal friends, credit card companies could probably save customers' lives by putting up a special reward for perpetrators who murder and steal cards.

IF YOU'RE TAKEN HOSTAGE

Comply with the criminal's demands until your first opportunity to escape or attack. Just do what they tell you until you get your chance. More victims wind up getting hurt when they don't resist.

Suppose your captor uses you as a shield while shooting at someone else. Act as if you have fainted. Dead weight is hard to carry along in a fire fight. Also, you become a smaller shield, which helps police marksmen to shoot without injuring you.

RECOGNIZING TROUBLE ON THE HORIZON

"Not long ago I spent an afternoon with a good friend. He's an experienced observer and hunter who seldom lacks sensitivity to his surroundings. He and his wife invited me to dinner at a great new Chinese restaurant. We drove in his $65,000 gray Mercedes.

In an area of closed businesses and run-down housing units, a motley looking crew of apparent gangsters looked us over from their corner at a traffic light. After a short discussion, four of the group started in our direction. I hit the door locks. 'Possible trouble on the right,' I said to my host. He gave no reaction—not even a glance.

While drawing my licensed handgun from my hip pocket, I noticed the light was still red. No help there. The approaching foursome split up. One pair came towards the right front door while the other pair moved around to the rear of the car. All four had hands thrust into coat pockets.

'We really ought to be moving along,' I warned.

'No hurry; our reservation isn't until 8:30.'

The group still on the corner was busy looking in all directions. Another pair stepped off the curb against the 'DON'T WALK' sign. They paused in the roadway where they could prevent us from making a right turn on the red.

Checking both directions and seeing no oncoming traffic I reached over, locked my left hand on the steering wheel and stepped down on my friend's accelerator foot. Amidst the gang's obscenities, we shot across the intersection. When I eased up about halfway down the next block, my friend was flabbergasted."

CLOCK CIRCLE
TO IDENTIFY DANGER

Your direction of travel 12

9   3

6   5
Danger here

Even though he is an intelligent man, the driver failed to do what most police departments now recommend: <u>Turn your perception knobs up</u>. In a sleazy section of a major East Coast city; in a car that screams '**I have money**;' he didn't even carry a weapon.

Note: Authors disagreed on the inclusion of the clock system for identifying danger. Although commonly used by professional bodyguards, Huber thought this system could cause confusion if you were not totally practiced and familiar with its use.

Here's the point. Most educated people wouldn't think of walking in a South American jungle at night. But, as anyone with jungle experience will tell you, <u>those jungles are much safer than our city streets.</u> If you want to be secure from crime, you have to assess the dangers out there realistically.

The best defense against violence is:
Avoid places where violence is most likely to occur.

Also, take advantage of the fact that you may have a friend with you. Whether you're walking on the street or driving in any kind of vehicle, warn each other of potentially dangerous situations. Tell your companion about your suspicions. Identify the location of the trouble so both of you know what you're talking about. As you travel, you move towards 12:00 o'clock, with three on your right and nine on your left. So---suppose you're being followed by a shady looking character off to your right. You say, "There's a creep following us at five o'clock 15 yards out." If you suspect anybody, <u>watch his hands</u>.

<u>WHAT CAN YOU DO ABOUT THE DANGER?</u>
The **DefCon** system may work best. Short for **Defense Cond**ition, it takes into account the seriousness of the danger, the probability of a crime occurring, (consider the neighborhood and your surroundings), the proximity of a suspicious attacker, and his movement and appearance.

If the situation feels bad, it probably is.

If the guy looks weird or out of place, he probably **is** trouble. Many macho people show off their tatoos and grow gross looking facial hair; their appearance is a display of rebellion. You need to decide if they are dangerous. You really do have a sixth sense; pay attention to it.

You have tasks to do as soon as you sense danger—-you prepare in stages. Maybe you sense danger when you can't really see or hear anything. That's your first notice, your warning order. Size things up. How many of the enemy? Are they focused on you? Are they within 10 yards?

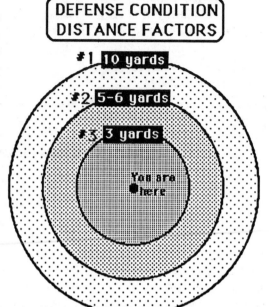

DEFENSE CONDITION DISTANCE FACTORS

#1 10 yards
#2 5-6 yards
#3 3 yards

You are here

If the answer to any of the above questions indicates trouble, you go to **DefCon 1.** Get control of your weapon and get it ready, address the problem by giving it your full and obvious attention, and look for a way to escape. Generally, robbers work in pairs; rapists work alone. Check behind you for a silent partner. Watch these people. Choose an escape route, or at least a place that gives you a defensive advantage. Perhaps it's a crowded store you can duck into, or some men you can ask for help. (Men in uniform, military, fire, police, security, etc, are generally trustworthy and may be helpful.)

DefCon 2 occurs after you have made tactical moves to avoid the problem, and the problem persists. It's now 5-6 yards away and closing in on you. You're closer to an escape route. Maybe you've moved towards help. You've double-surveyed your area 360° to check for additional trouble. Your plan of defense is clear, and you're getting ready. Your weapon is now ready to fire or spray but still hidden (in a purse, under a newspaper, or in your pocket).

SAFETY AND
SECURITY INFORMATION

As our guest, your safety is important to us. We encourage you to take advantage of the following suggestions to help make your stay more enjoyable:

• Safeguard your room key at all times.

• Use the deadbolt and security bar/chain on the door whenever you are in your room. Also, be sure that sliding glass doors and connecting room doors are locked.

• Check to be sure your room door closes properly when you leave your room.

• Use the "peep hole" on the door to identify persons who knock. Never open the door until you are positive of who it is. If you have any questions about the person or his/her purpose, contact the front desk. All hotel employees wear a uniform and name badge.

• Familiarize yourself with the fire safety information and procedures posted on the back of your room door. Report smoke or fire immediately to the front desk (dial "0"), or to the fire department (dial "9-1-1").

• Place your valuables in the hotel's safe deposit boxes at the front desk. Do not leave valuables in your room or vehicle.

• Use the hotel's main entrance if you are returning late in the evening. Other entrances may be locked.

• Report any suspicious activities or persons to the front desk.

• Observe all posted rules when using the swimming pool and other recreational facilities.

Hampton Inn ®

MEMPHIS, TENNESSEE (800) 423-1020 (901) 362-9239

At about 3 yards, with things getting progressively worse, you'll have to make an offensive move. Take a stand. Get control of the situation. You can say, "Stop right there! You people scare me. If you want to avoid severe pain, turn around and leave now!" This is **DefCon 3**, and the next step is shoot. Once you've issued a warning, you have a right to be afraid. Fear for your life is grounds to spray gas, attack with a non-shooting weapon, or let lead fly. When all your DefCon 3 options have been used, go to war. Win decisively.

STAYING AWARE
Knowledge and awareness of your surroundings are critical ingredients of any self-defense plan. <u>Always pay attention to what is going on.</u> When driving, listen to the news. A police scanner in your car can warn you of trouble ahead. When at home listen for telltale sounds indicating trouble. A squeaky door, floorboards creaking, or the sound of broken glass should alert you. In an enclosed space, learn a trick from karate instructors: Don't stare ahead at one point; soften your focus. Train yourself to see everything 180° in front of you.

Don't situate yourself so you look into the sun outdoors or into bright lights indoors. The idea is to observe; not to be observed. Don't turn up your television, stereo or car radio so loud you can't hear what is going on. The idea is to hear; not to make a lot of noise. Head phones make you deaf to your surroundings and kill your ability to sense danger. You can let your guard down in one area of the country without a problem, but the same relaxation could get you quickly killed just a few miles down the road.

Besides being cautious, show restraint in dress. Don't display wealth or expensive jewelry. Wear gloves over your rings until you're out of sight of the casual observer, the parking lot attendant, the cab driver, or the ticket taker at the opera. Many of those people sell information. They're part time, hired for one night only, and sometimes go after those kinds of jobs just for the extra money they can make from the information they pass along.

To become less of a target, develop a lower profile. Season tickets to the opera or ball game in your name could be trouble. Certainly, don't have tickets sent to your home address. The list of season ticket holders is frequently sold for six cents a name. Temporary employees could market the list on their own to any organization (Burglary, Inc.). The person who goes to the opera every Thursday is an easy mark for house burglars. Buy tickets in the name of the company for which you work and take delivery elsewhere than your home——your business address or a rental post office box address.

MAIL AND ADDRESS SECURITY
Your home address should appear on none of your personal identification. Get a privately owned mail box (Mail Boxes Etc.) or at least a post office box address and use that on your driver's license and vehicle registration. If it isn't that way now, fill out a form and change it. Thus, whoever steals your wallet doesn't get your home address. Use the same mailing address on your car keys. With name and true home address on your key ring, loss or theft makes it easy for thieves to invade your home. Likewise, use your mail box address on baggage labels at airports. Why? Baggage handlers have been known to sell information to house burglars---who would just love to know you'll be gone for a few weeks.

IS YOUR OFFICE IN YOUR HOME?
Many people claiming a deduction for office in home are now audited by IRS. Therefore, many have moved into office space which has given rise to a new industry. Often called, "Executive Suites," smart operators lease a large commercial building, divide it into smaller office space, and

furnish a wide variety of perks and benefits to lessees. The building is fairly secure. Some are guarded. Mail can be safely sent to this address. Your phone is answered professionally and voice mail takes over when you're not in your office. Federal Express and UPS stop there, and outgoing mail and FAX is also provided. All of this can mean more security, and it doesn't cost very much.

More and more, people shop by phone with a credit card across state lines as state sales taxes increase. (Some states collect no sales tax on out-of-state deliveries.) Never give your home address to any stranger, especially over the phone. Take delivery at your rented mail box address.

PHONE SECURITY
Every phone conversation you have with friends should include an, " I'm OK" code message. If you were kidnapped or taken hostage in your home, the perpetrators will let you answer the phone but monitor the conversation closely, often at gun point. So, you might say, "Buddy's doing fine," which means: Everything's all right. Without you delivering that message over the phone, it means, "I'm in trouble and I need help right away." Thus, you can warn someone without saying anything.

Also, <u>be careful</u> over the cellular phone. Many scanners can be programmed to cellular channels so criminal eaves-droppers can routinely listen in. Some sell information.

INCREASE YOUR SECURITY AS YOUR WEALTH BUILDS
In our opinion, any person with a substantial amount of wealth **must** employ at least simple security measures. That was the failure of New York millionaire Harvey Weinstein---who was kidnapped and dumped in a hole in the ground for over a week before being rescued. Apparently, he trusted one of his employees, but he also developed a routine which made him predictable. SAVE, Survivors Against Violent Encounters, sent him a complimentary copy of our first edition after his rescue. August 93.

VARY YOUR ACTIVITY

Don't establish easily observed patterns of travel and activity. Interested thieves keep notes on your arrival and departures. Don't drive the same route every day; take as many different routes as possible to work and school. Leave and return at different times. Computers and modems are creating new home employment opportunities. Any time you can work at home instead of the office, you decrease your exposure.

Discussing your wealth with strangers or casual acquaintances is very poor security. Referencing your Mercedes, your summer home, or 'Daddy's little ole factory' are all poor choices for casual conversation with any but your closest friends. While we're at it, don't reserve any parking space anywhere in your own name. Use a code name, the same way you should on your credit cards. For the management staff at Disneyland, for example, who just made millions of dollars, I recommend labelling the spaces with Mickey Mouse, Goofey etc, and rotating the names every so often. Otherwise, anybody with a pair of binoculars can find out the bosses' license numbers, trace the car to the house, or set up a kidnap while the car is in transit.

Engrave everything you own with your social security number and/or your driver's license number. Fences pay less for traceable property. Thieves have been known to leave engraved goods alone. Also, police catch thieves and recover thousands in stolen goods. If engraved, you get them back and the prosecution's case is stronger. If not, you can buy them at a police auction; the perp gets off.

Trust nobody. Today, police departments hire some bad apples. With all the drug money around, temptation is tremendous. In Kailua, Oahu, Hawaii, the police department discovered several officers connected with burglars and stolen property. Some resigned; newspapers never published the names of the others. In San Diego, an attorney who was president of the local Bar Association was indicted for receiving stolen property. He was a fence. In New York, Oct 93, a police officer testified under oath that he had stolen drugs and sold them, stolen money, and even raided a brothel, in which he forced prostitutes to have sex with him after kicking johns out of bed. Said Serpico, (of movie fame) about this recent corruption, "It goes all the way to the top."

Never give a parking lot attendant or auto service man your complete key ring. With the parking lot attendant, only the ignition key is necessary. It's far better to arrange to park the car yourself and keep your keys. House keys left in trust with your neighbor get no ID tag. An enterprising thief in your neighbor's home would pocket your key for future use, of course.

DAYTIME BURGLARY, OWNER DECOYED
In the "Gypsy Scenario," a friendly, presentable-looking individual, quite often an attractive young women, approaches you in your front yard and asks to speak with your wife. She appears to be taking a survey. If your wife is not home, or if she comes out of the house to speak to the young lady, a signal of some kind tells the young lady's accomplice to enter the house on the opposite side and spend five minutes gathering up valuables.

When at home or in your yard, keep all doors locked. When outdoors, keep a cordless phone with you so you can call 911. Then wait for police to come and search your house for a hidden burglar. Warn them, "I believe there's a burglar in this house. Would you search while I wait outside?"

Be careful about going into your house if things are not exactly as you left them. An open door into your house may draw you in to a burglary in progress, and 50% of these situations turn out to be violent. Call for help and don't touch anything. The same with your car. If the doors are open (they should always be locked), be careful. Check for stow-away germs and people close by, whom you may have surprised.

Consider three time frames in any defense plan: *Before, during, and after*. The police don't handle "before" a crime is committed. Rarely can the police arrive "during" a crime. Taking a report is routine; sometimes, even that doesn't work too well. In many areas, county sheriffs and city police don't cooperate. Even though you live in the city, police won't take a report on a theft you think occurred in the county. Sheriffs' crime reports often don't filter in to police information output. Political infighting and bitterness between elected officials puts you more at risk than ever.

The *before* and *during* time frames of a crime are up to you. The steps you take *before* a crime occurs may make the difference between your living unmolested in peace or becoming a victim. Use the time you have *before* to plan what will happen *during.* That way, you lessen the chances of qualifying for police assistance---by first becoming a victim. Once you formulate your plan and practice, your life should go along smoothly with little interference from the criminal germs and viruses prowling our streets.

FELONY CONVICTION = LOSS OF WELFARE

Would the crime rate go down if criminals knew they would lose welfare? Maybe a conviction should cancel entitlements, rent subsidies, etc.

Gun control laws will never reduce violent crime. Only law-abiding citizens will obey gun control laws---something a criminal will never do. Criminals are for gun control because it would improve working conditions. With gun control, the slogan, "Fight crime; shoot back," will mean nothing.

Chapter 2

FORTIFYING YOUR CASTLE

Burglary! It's **big business**. In California alone, burglars stole a reported 864 million dollars worth of property in 1991. When police announce they have just broken a burglary ring operating for the last five years, take note. Many small American businesses fold after operating for less than a year, so a five-year run is a success story. When you factor in the cost of police efforts to put burglars out of business, either the burglars are doing something right, or the criminal justice system isn't . .

The average home in America is a pushover for any amateur burglar. Approximately 50% of burglars enter through an unlocked door or window. Others come in via an open garage. Your house may be locked, but if the garage is open, the burglar enters, shuts the garage door, and uses the owner's tools to break in through a wall. You can purchase remote controlled dead bolt locks for your garage door. But, **don't** remote these to the same frequency as your garage door opener.

Also, from now on, never leave your house unless a radio or TV talk show is on. It makes it sound as if someone's home. You can't make your house absolutely impregnable, but when you make your house just a little harder to break into than your neighbors' houses, you've probably eliminated 90% of possible break-ins.

IF YOU MOVE TO A NEW AREA

Be careful in your choice of neighborhoods. A cul de sac neighborhood with only one access street is far less appealing to criminals. A neighborhood with security fencing and a guarded entrance is great.

The high risk for attack by professional house breakers is between 9:00 in the morning and 2:00 in the afternoon. People are generally at work or at school during these hours and a delivery or service van elicits little suspicion from the neighbors. An area where some folks have retired and remained in place is a great deal better than one where all the adults are away all day. Retired folks grew up during a time when honesty and property rights were respected. They don't have a regular schedule to keep, love to walk around the neighborhood at odd times, and notice most everything going on.

For even tighter security, form a **Neighborhood Defense Team**. With an NDT communications net, patrolling members (in pairs, often with a dog) can use hand held radios to call for help. While on patrol, team members can also use cellular phones with a roster of neighbors' numbers in the memory so they can check on visitors or intruders. NDT means criminals can't even get into your neighborhood. You'll be much safer when you band together with neighbors, develop specialists, and tie your patrols into central communication.

Other considerations would include: a neighborhood away from the main stream of urban traffic, but one that is not remote from police, fire department, ambulance and other emergency services. The house itself shouldn't be secluded. It should be easily seen from the street by passing police patrols and easily observed by your immediate neighbors.

FORTIFICATION

Just as in the federal budget, defense should be an on-going item in your own monthly budget. Spend so much per month for groceries, so much for defense, etc. It's the price of peace. Thus, your house keeps getting safer.

Newly developed security devices enable you to make your castle better-fortified every month. If you ever sell, you'll recapture investment.

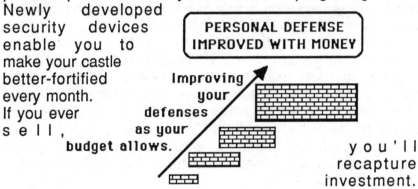

Every bit of protection you add keeps you further away from violent conflict and invasion. The average burglary costs you over $2,500, so adding extra protection to your home on a regular basis is a great idea.

new move ins.

CHANGE YOUR LOCKS

No matter what your dwelling, a mobile home, an apartment, condo or house, change the locks! Contact a bonded locksmith or just pull your old locks out and visit a hardware store for a replacement. Do this the day you move in. Replace **all** the locks in your home. Most new house builders use cheap locks. But you can get a door lock which can't be picked. Police estimate that 25% of apartment burglary comes from managers and building superintendents with a key. If you bought a new house, replace the locks. Ask the builder how many extra keys are floating around. "Well let's see now, the plumber had to have one, the floor guy, oh yeah and the guy who said he was with the exterminator company." Did the builder get all of the keys back? Sure. . ! In addition to installing new locks, install double key, dead bolt locks on outside doors and on the door connecting the garage and house. Key these locks the same as the door locks.

> **WHAT ABOUT HOUSE KEYS?** Most homeowners leave a spare key within arms reach of the door. Burglars know this! Hide a key where you can't be seen retrieving it. Also, never leave your keys in plain sight inside the house, especially near a window with burglar bars on it. (They'll reach through with a fishing pole.)

Changing locks is a priority item because it's a defense **against night intrusion**. Most simple burglary happens during the day. Usually, professional house burglars are not much of a personal threat; they generally try to avoid occupied homes. The real pros will often let themselves be caught rather than risk injuring or killing someone, or getting shot themselves.

. WHO'S THERE? PROFESSIONAL THIEF, OR WORSE?
However, if someone breaks into your house at night, while you're at home, you should assume this is serious—probably deadly—trouble. It could mean rape, robbery at gun point to support a drug habit, or murder. Whoever breaks in is either prepared to kill or do severe bodily harm, especially when cornered. You must consider the situation to be the worst and act accordingly. This is the gravest extreme; be mentally prepared to take violent action in defense of your family. Don't try to wound; wounding shots are aimed towards extremities, and therefore often miss completely.*

> *   Most law enforcement agencies have an unwritten policy regarding the use of wounding (to disable) violent subjects. Don't! If an individual is armed and posing a threat to anyone, shoot to kill! Shooting to wound **can** kill---you, because you may miss.
>
> Officers involved in fatal shootings are instructed to testify to the fact they were shooting to "incapacitate" or to "neutralize" a subject or threat. Death of the perpetrator usually does that.

IF YOU GO AWAY ON VACATION, ETC.

Try your best to make it look and sound as if someone is home. A device on your lamp will turn the lights on and off at random times. Leave a radio playing on a talk station. Close some of the blinds so a burglar hunting for his next victim has to worry about what he can't see. Ask your neighbor to park his car in your driveway during your absence. **Don't** allow mail, flyers, newspapers, etc. to build up in front of your house. If you return to an opened home, never enter. Go to a neighbor and call police.

LIGHT UP THE NIGHT

Install lights. Several retail outlets sell a security light which turns on automatically when something moves in front of its eye. Put these on all four sides of your home. They also work well on an RV. You'll probably never know the number of actual peeping toms, burglars and other real intruders the lights scare away.

Another inexpensive item to consider is the two-way, four- station intercom. Battery powered, they work equally well in any recreational vehicle. With one of the remote speakers mounted near your front door, you don't have to open the door or look through the peephole to see who is there. You can operate this 9-volt battery-powered wonder from the safety of your bedroom sanctuary. If you turn up the volume, you can hear close whispering or a conversation out in the street.

Heavy duty safety chains on all outside doors help, but anybody for whom you open the door just a crack can cut most chains in seconds with a small bolt cutter. The newer model chains are made with case-hardened steel, but even if the chain holds, the screws may not. Long, stainless steel screws are best. If you pre-drill the holes, squirt glue into them before you run the screws in for maximum protection.

Next, replace all the window latches. Builders who use cheap door hardware use cheaper window latches. Good locks, strong latches and hinges are the cheapest insurance you can buy. Sad to say, though, you can't depend on strong locks alone.

Once your locks and latches are replaced, you've eliminated a good percentage of burglaries. For even more security in your home, you have to do something about the windows. Various grades of shatter resistant glass are available, but they're expensive and none withstand repeated blows from a heavy hammer or crow bar. To secure the glass, install attractive decorative window and door grill work such as you see in Mexico and South America. When you install these units, make sure you can release them from inside in case you need to escape from your home. Fire, and sometimes aggressive intruders will cause you to flee. From second story windows, a chain ladder is a good idea.

Don't think you've won the war after you install grills. Criminals have taught me how to go fishin'. With a pole and a hook, they can reach in through the bars on any open window and snag a purse, wallet, **keys,** or anything else within eight feet. Besides the fishing pole technique, the same people teach little kids how to unlock doors from the inside. They slip the child through the window bars, and then walk in through an opened door.

If you don't like grills, try storm windows. They add to the security of your home and also reduce the cost of heating and cooling by as much as 25%. Also, alarm screens work well. You can leave your screened windows open all day or night and still be protected. Internal movement, light or sound won't set these off; it takes tampering from the outside.

Install solid wood or insulated metal doors rather than hollow-core junk. When you install solid-core doors, ask the door builder to rout in another cut for an extra hinge or two. If your Neighborhood Defense Team engineer is helping or installing the doors for you, consider a layer of Kevlar. That way, you can stand near the door without fear of incoming bullets harming you. Kevlar or other bullet proofing is a must if you build the door with a firing port in it and cover that port with a see-through mirror. Naturally, you must have all your hinge pins accessible only from the inside. When you install your hinges, drill deep into the door and use screws—extra long and strong. Glass insets for exterior doors invite burglars. All they have to do is wrap a hand in heavy cloth and punch through, then reach through the hole to open the door from the inside. If you want to keep the glass, then install deadbolt locks which can only be unlocked from either side with a key; of course, don't leave the key in the lock.

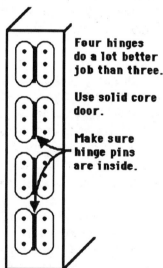

Four hinges do a lot better job than three.

Use solid core door.

Make sure hinge pins are inside.

Avoid sliding glass doors. They provide easy access routes into your home and are difficult to secure. Where these doors are already in place build a grill to cover the entire unit. At least install a drop stick to keep them from these doors are already in place build a grill to cover the entire unit. At least install a drop stick to keep them from being forced open from the outside. Better, buy two or more locking gadgets. Then put sensors on them when you install your Transcience electronic break-in detection system.

Purchase an inexpensive revolving yellow light for the roof of your house, and remote switch this to the inside of your sanctuary. If you call the police, flip the switch; it will save them from having to look for a house number. Tell the police dispatcher your revolving yellow light is on; that message will go out over the radio. Another way: use a special switch for porch or street number lights. Flip it once to turn them on. Flip twice to make them blink.

FOUR-FOOTED BODYGUARDS
USING ANIMALS FOR PROTECTION

Even before you install good locks, bright lights and grill work, **get a dog.** Any dog! Big, mean-looking dogs are great, but little, loud, dogs are good too. Dogs not only make your home less attractive to burglars, they're also great for letting you know if there is some other life-threatening problem. They smell smoke well before most electronic smoke detectors do, and they sense big storms long before arrival. Dogs can be neutralized in a number of ways. But the time it takes for an assailant to deal with your dog may give you precious time to escape or shoot.

Defensive dogs come in two varieties, attack dogs and guard dogs. You can teach a dog to attack on command. To get that kind of dog trained, you normally need to spend between $500 and $1,000 with a trainer. When the dog is about 6 months old, a trainer will teach obedience, and then offensive tactics. Though the idea may be appealing, that's not what you need.

The second variety of dog guards your house or vehicle. They also need obedience school, and you should take them yourself. The more time you spend with your dog, the more the dog will be devoted to you. When the dog is still young, it's a good idea to pay strangers to invade his territory and run away when he barks and charges. Praise it lavishly after it attempts to protect your territory. Pretty soon the dog gets the idea to protect your yard, your house, and your car anytime you ask.

WHAT BREED?

Unless you have a great deal of time and money to spend, I don't recommend the traditional guard dogs for the sole purpose of home defense. Mixed breeds cost less and have a tendency to be more physically stable than many of the larger registered canines. The mixed breeds I've known have displayed admirable levels of determination and a willingness to do battle. A trained dog becomes a valuable and integral part of your home defense system. This will be hard to do, but keep the dog at an emotional distance. If trouble occurs, never put yourself at risk to try to save the dog. In most cases the dog is better equipped to defend himself than you are. You might also confuse the dog or get in its way, thereby limiting its ability to defend itself.

SIGNS FOR SECURITY

HOME PROTECTED BY SUPERIOR ALARM CO. Yeah, burglarize this house; you'll set off an alarm. QUIET PLEASE. DAY SLEEPER. Announces that someone is at home all day. PROPERTY UNDER VIDEO SURVEILLANCE, tells a burglar to smile; he's on candid camera. DO YOU BELIEVE IN LIFE AFTER DEATH? TRESPASS IN THIS HOUSE AND FIND OUT FOR SURE. Finally, THIS HOME IS PROTECTED BY SHOTGUN THREE NIGHTS A WEEK. YOU GUESS WHICH THREE.

CHAIN LINK FENCING

Chain-link fence (6 ft.) and gates at the driveway are a great security addition to any property. That's why our government installs so much chain-link fence. Nothing is better. Set the posts deep into concrete. A single strand of electric fencing on top can be shocking.

Don't use solid wood or brick wall fencing. These give thieves and other outlaws a hiding place. Five-foot-high, split rail fencing backed with 2x4 mesh "horse wire" makes a sturdy, attractive, hard-to-climb fence. A single strand of barbed wire wrapped loosely around the top rail of such a fence increases security. Don't set anything outside your fence which would make the fence easy to climb.

EVEN WITHOUT FENCING

DRIVEWAY SECURITY

PILLARS FROM BRICK AND A LOCKING GATE

For your driveway, attractive stone or brick pillars allow you to hang lockable gates. This deprives thieves of vehicle access to your possessions. They don't like to carry heavy TV's across the yard to a vehicle. (If they weren't so lazy they might not be thieves.) Besides, they don't want to be seen. If you are part of a defense team, you'll have patrols in your neighborhood. The patrols will be able to close your gate and lock it anytime.

Invest in a safe deposit box at your local bank. Keep all your expensive jewelry, negotiable bonds, insurance papers, rare coins and other highly portable and disposable valuables in the box. Let anyone who asks about your valuables know you don't keep them in your home. Where you do keep them is nobody's business.

Make an inventory of your possessions. Estimate what it would cost to replace them; then insure them for full value. Most people are surprised to find out how much they've accumulated. Unfortunately, most people don't discover this until they're filling out insurance claims.

YOUR VAULT

Build your own security room or vault. The best locations are in a corner of your house—-on either the second floor or in the basement. A basement corner where the walls are back-filled on the outside is the most secure and the easiest conversion. Once built, it will be a strong, hard-to-violate security locker.

Use 2 x 6 studs. At waist height and perhaps other places, drill the studs and set rebar in through the holes. Cover both sides of the walls with diagonal 2 X 6. (If you use surplus lumber, treat for insects.) Next, solid sheet both sides with heavy duty plywood. Glue that plywood to the diagonal

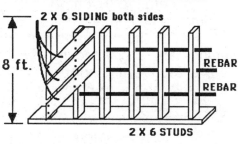

BUILDING YOUR OWN HOME VAULT

2 X 6 SIDING both sides

8 ft.

REBAR

REBAR

2 X 6 STUDS

Cover with plywood, both sides

2 X 6 with panel adhesive and nail it on with screw nails. Panel or paint the inside. Hang a steel insert or solid core door only an archangel with Tomb of Jesus experience could penetrate. On four hinges, hang the door so the hinge pins are inside. This makes it nearly impossible for someone to force the door open or to tear it away from the frame. Put two (same key) dead bolts on it, one located a foot from the top of the door and the other located a foot and a half from the bottom. Use battery operated lights. You can build your vault for less than the cost of a home safe. At the same time, you get five to ten times the secure storage space. Steel gun safes are still a worthwhile investment for storing cameras, silver, jewelry and firearms. For double protection, put your gun safe into your home-built security vault.

stays less than five minutes in a home. To save the farm, all you have to do is make it unprofitable after five minutes of collecting. Leave a decoy; once he thinks he's scored, he's out of there. Attend a business auction and buy an old safe. Hide it where a thief can discover it easily, and store some precious junk and fakes in it. Perhaps you'll include a few pieces of costume jewelry, a stack of stock certificates from defunct companies, a sack of small coins.

MARKING YOUR POSSESSIONS

Inventory everything in your home and take pictures. Make a detailed inventory list. Keep serial numbers and receipts for purchase together in a safe place. Record every item's serial number and put your name, driver's license number, and social security number on your possessions to help a recovering agency find you. If you can't prove ownership of stolen property, the perp often goes free and you don't get your property back.

THE SANCTUARY OR, SAFE ROOM

Any room providing you with an additional level of security serves as a sanctuary in your home. The best choice is a bedroom with a commanding view of the head of the stairs or the hall separating sleeping quarters from the rest of the home. Most often, that's your own master bedroom. Usually, it has a phone and a bathroom you can use as an inner sanctum with its own source of water and first aid gear. Take into account exceptional circumstances. Is there a handicapped member in your family? Maybe you'll use that person's room for a sanctuary or move the person to your master bedroom.

Children often become aware of danger on their own. Teach them to go to the sanctuary when in danger. Be sure to acquaint your baby sitters with the sanctuary concept and defense procedures. Pay special attention to window security in your sanctuary. On the ground floor, or if easily reached from any place on the roof, install stout grills on security in your sanctuary. On the ground floor, or if easily reached from any place on the roof, install stout grills on sanctuary windows. For windows two stories high with no outside access, include a chain or rope ladder so you can escape. Install solid core doors with dead bolt locks to make these areas secure. A cross bolt drop-in 2 X 4 makes the doors battering ram proof.

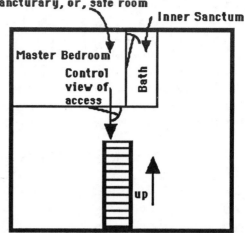

Sanctuary, or, safe room

Inner Sanctum

Master Bedroom
Control
view of
access
Bath
up

Not the best floor plan. Attacking germ can kick through wallboard to gain access to bathroom which would be better on outside corner of the house.

Our favorite home alarm system starts for around $600. Save on installation; do it yourself. Most companies look at your floor plan and tell you exactly where to locate and install everything. Once installed, you'll feel as if you live in a well-guarded fortress.

Don't keep valuables in your sanctuary. You don't want to draw a threat to that area. Instead, use the wealth stored elsewhere in your home as a bargaining chip to gain time while you wait for help. If you have weapons in the home and are trained, they should be loaded and ready.

Solid Core Door
THREAT 2 X 4 SAFE
Iron Angle
Hinges to Safe Side

Since a high percentage of home invasions while the owner is present turn violent, make this announcement:

"Listen carefully; there is nothing of value stored in this area of the house. There is a safe downstairs, and the combination is 36-12-25. Take what you want and leave. If you come towards this area, **we** will kill you." Never let on to someone who has broken into your home that you're alone. Examples: "We," not "I" and, "Our," not "My." This is the best time to chamber a round into your shotgun. All felons know, understand, and respect that sound.

In addition to your self defense weapons, store two top quality flashlights with extra bulbs and batteries in your sanctuary. If you have a portable cellular phone, keep that in the sanctuary with you, too.

Except defense firearms, store weapons in your vault room or gun safe. Store bolt action rifles with the bolts removed and semi-automatic pistols with the slides removed from the frames. Ammo is stored separately. Put the bolts and slides in a separate locking storage box. Therefore, the weapons can't readily be used against you or a future victim. An unfireable weapon is just so much scrap metal, both to the thief and the fence who buys from him.

THE INNER SANCTUM

Within your sanctuary, you need a special place where your children and others can wait out the intrusion and be safe from attack. With an extra layer of protection between them and danger, they'll be out of harm's way. Nobody comes out of the Inner Sanctum until you give them a pre-arranged signal. If you get into trouble, they'll have to tough it out until help arrives. Either a large walk-in closet or a bathroom will suffice. Just as with your sanctuary, pay special attention to the solid core door and window. Hinges must be on the safe side (inside) of the room. If you've trained one of your children on a weapon, that weapon is stored in the inner sanctum.

> New York and Washington D.C. have the "best" gun controls. They also have the highest crime rates.

SECONDARY SAFE ROOM

In a large home or one with several floors it's a good idea to establish a second safe room close to where you spend most of your time. Set the second safe room up like the first. You'll want extra insulation between you and a threat, a strong door and good lock, and a defense weapon secure and well hidden, but loaded and handy. Put a phone in this room also.

WORKMEN IN YOUR HOME

On street corners all over America, someone who looks a little disheveled stands with a sign that says, "WILL WORK FOR FOOD." It's a good business for many. One person in Florida was recently killed so that the murderer could take over his corner, on which he made $200 a day. The scam often goes like this: "I'm really a willing worker. Just let me come to your house; I can fix anything." Then later, he comes back and steals everything in sight. If he gets caught, he says, "They hired me and didn't pay me." Even if the explanation doesn't work and he goes to jail, he's gotten what he wanted.

When real workers come to install or fix anything, keep your valuables out of sight. Stay at home while the installation is being made and keep an eye on the crew. Find out how long they have been with the company. Before you decide on a company, find out if its bond covers the installation and service personnel against theft. One more note on employees in your home: Choose baby sitters carefully; it's like building anything---measure twice, cut once. Interview baby sitters carefully and check references. Any doubts? Install a VAR (Voice Activated Tape Recorder) with multiple pick-up mikes for about $50. You'll be able to hear a recording of all the noise in your house while you're away, including phone calls, baby sitter visits from boyfriends, parties, or child abuse. **Do not employ strangers in your home.** Bonded workers only; thank you. Stay near the workmen---and watch.

APARTMENT SECURITY

Apartment dwellers may face different problems. Ideally an apartment house would have enclosed parking with limited access and TV monitoring of the parking area, the entrance and hallways. The next best thing is to have outside doors that lock automatically. Do away with electric latch systems that allow lazy neighbors to unlock the main door without bothering to see who is there. Convicted rapists, child abductors and burglars have explained: They like those buildings because tenants inside feel the false security and often let down their guard. So the perps stand on the entry doorstep with a story and keep on ringing until someone lets them in.

Middle floor apartments are the easiest to secure. With a three story apartment building, the most secure location is a corner unit on the second floor without direct access to a fire escape. Don't visit your apartment laundry room at night alone. Lots of crime, (rape) occurs there.

Make sure all doors to the outside or hallway are solid core construction and add the extra hinge. The alarm system is just as viable for apartment dwellers as any other home owner.

You're most vulnerable to attack as you leave or arrive at your home or business. Be especially watchful

a. from the time you exit your place of business until you're in your vehicle with doors locked.

b. from the time you exit your vehicle until inside your home.

Be observant, and ready to run (or fight), depending on the circumstances. A mistake when you're tired at the end of a long drive can put you in the real estate business in three days. They'll give you a small bit of land, a marble marker, and free advertising--in the obituaries.

YOU'RE AT RISK HERE: IN YOUR OWN GARAGE

We're highly in favor of electric garage door openers, electric gates, or both. Garages are often hiding places for kids who take drugs. Worse, they hide attackers or burglars from street view. Can you imagine the trouble you'd be in when out of the car, (while running) and opening your door?

Put a bright bulb in your garage opener. You want to flood the garage with light. Don't leave any place in the garage set up so someone could hide in there and wait for you. Put the door down as soon as you park and before you unlock your car doors, especially at night.

RIOTS AND NATURAL DISASTERS

In the face of a natural disaster, or if your neighborhood is embroiled in a civil disturbance, are you going to evacuate or stay and fight? Hurricane Andrew demolished Homestead, Florida. Even before the winds quit, looters were taking advantage of the victims, just hit by disaster, and stealing the last of all they had.

Set up a grab-and-run bag packed for each family member and a family weekender bag packed with extra clothing, food and first aid gear. Pack the bag with standard outdoor gear. (See *GREAT LIVIN' IN GRUBBY TIMES.*) If you are trained, pack a defense weapon, ammo, and some form of currency. In my exterior frame backpack, I like the compartments so I know where everything is located. Various compartments contain a water purifier, binoculars, a .357 mag with lots of ammo, several kinds of knives, parachute cord, two hammocks, and some canned goods for food. MRE's (Meals, Ready to Eat) weigh less. I also carry a survival .22 rifle which breaks down and floats. No matter where I go, I know I can stay a while.

If your strategy will be to leave in the event of disaster or riot, make sure your escape vehicle's tank never drops below half. Keep some extra gas in a safe storage area.

Use that fuel and replace it again every six months or so. At the first sign of trouble, get out. Don't wait until the rioters are on your block to move. Get at least 25 miles away; perhaps get a motel room. Notify your entire family and the police about your departure. If you have time before you leave, secure all your valuables in your vault room. No vault room? Put your goodies in your bathroom, push the lock button on the inside and close the door. Turn on a battery powered radio in that room to a talk station. Leave your TV on. Do the most you can to make looters think somebody's home.

As you continue to implement these instructions, you'll be safer. Work on security; keep making your home safer. Most alarm companies sell improvements and upgrades you can make as you have the cash and time to add them on. Transcience, for example, sells door sensors and panic buttons to make their system even better. Once you have the alarm installed, you can add these items later.

The money you spend on various projects to keep you and your family safe from tragedy is the best investment you can make. But it's difficult to comprehend the benefit you gain when you never become a victim. Perhaps you'll appreciate the money you invest when a crime occurs down the street. The victim: someone who just bought a large entertainment system instead of a security device. The day she decided not to make her home as secure as yours, she became a target.

WHAT SHOULD A CONVICT LOSE?

What about a loss in civil rights? Once convicted of a crime, we know who they are and what they do, so their right to remain silent after arrest should no longer exist. Any utterance over the phone could be used. Technical laws on search and seizure which would toss evidence against them would no longer apply. Anything found in their possession should be used against them in prosecution, no matter how obtained. After all, aren't we at war with criminals?

Chapter 3

NON-SHOOTING WEAPONS

The idea is to avoid conflict if you can, but make sure you don't lose any fights you can't avoid. **In conflict with a criminal, any weapon is better than no weapon.**

Weapons, however don't make you invincible. They just help. By definition, a weapon is only an extension of your fighting ability. If you arm yourself with a twenty-pound baseball bat, (beyond your fighting ability), some gorilla will simply take it away from you. Also, don't face up to a firearm with a stick. When the germs have a gun, just about any weapon you choose could cause you to finish in second place. Understand also, that if you use a firearm in the face of a threat not considered lethal, you could face prosecution.

Weapons other than firearms definitely have a place in your defense structure. In some areas, it's not legal to carry a gun. In many cases, people buy a firearm and toss it in a drawer; then they get into a confrontation without practice and training. Remember, once you introduce a firearm into a conflict, you elevate it to lethal. Even if you shoot in unquestionable, absolute self defense, you might still be guilty of crime. Finally, you might not be armed when the need arises, so knowing how to defend yourself with something other than a firearm is important.

Let's consider your options. To do that, first understand the elements of combat. Before you choose a weapon, consider **range, speed, power, control, target accuracy, and operational convenience.** Apply these elements to your own strength and ability.

Range. This term defines the distance to a given target. If you keep an opponent away from you, but still close enough for you to reach out and smack with feeling, you win. Examples: Your legs are longer than his arms so you can kick; your sword or spear is longer than his knife; your Bo (five-foot hardwood shaft) will reach out better than a short club. In this chapter, we'll be discussing long range and short range weapons. The longer the range, the safer you'll be. You risk personal injury any time you get in close to an assailant.

Speed. Quickness counts a lot. If you can move faster than your opponent, you'll score and do some damage before he does. So, a weapon enabling you to strike fast is a good idea. For example, you can jab with your Bo, so the blow lands before a block can deflect it. Note also, you have to be fast enough to get your Bo back out of there before he can grab. Don't choose a weapon you can't control. Lose your weapon in a fight and your assailant gains the advantage you thought you had.

Power. You have to deliver sufficient force with a blow to make your influence felt. A severe bruise or opened blood vessel generally means you've done damage (as opposed to only pain). On the other hand, minor bruise or pain merely gets your opponent's adrenaline flowing.

Target accuracy. All assailants have delicate target areas. Hitting hard on his shoulder won't help you much. But the same force to the throat or groin helps him to see things your way. Some weapons are easier to direct accurately on a desired body target than others. The target body consists of pain producing points, damage producing points, and fatal areas. Take your pick.

Operational convenience. Does it take two hands or one to make your weapon work for you? Can you make it readily available or do you have to unpack and unfold it? How much muscle do you need to cause this weapon to work righteously on your criminal target? If only one hand is required, can you use a separate weapon in the other?

Now, let's examine several options in the light of combat principles. Take a personal inventory. Whether you're tall and strong or short and weak, some kinds of weapons will work best for you. You can either make one or purchase one.

DEFENSIVE SPRAY GAS
Spraying gas is the best way to counter an attack if you don't want to shoot somebody. It's also favored because it reaches out to handle the problem before an assailant gets in close. You can get CN gas (tear gas--- immediate gratification) or CS gas (slower acting, but more effective chocking gas), or a pepper formula, which temporarily blinds your assailant. For under $20, don't leave home without spray gas, unless you fly by commercial air where depressurization can cause a gas leak in your

suitcase. Spray is one of the better women's defense tools. You don't need to be strong, and you can hit from a distance. You need only one hand. For excellent results, choose a CS gas mixed with a blend of pepper. It's fast acting because of the evaporating additives it contains. The manufacturer claims "instant action," and we believe that.

KEY CHAINS KEYED TO DEFENSE

At most Army/Navy surplus stores, you can buy a Makiwara stick (a short, fist-sized stick which attaches to your key chain). To use these sticks effectively, you need some karate training because you'll need to snap in order to penetrate a target body. Even if you're no expert, the sticks provide a handle for your key chain. Therefore, you always have them with you. If you're untrained, you can use the stick as a handle for a one ounce fishing sinker installed on your key ring. The sinker is a great persuader.

MEASURING THE STAFF OF LIFE FOR A STREET FIGHTER

Proper length for the Bo

LONG RANGE HELP

The Bo. Usually, you make yours as long as you are, but not wider than the inside of your car so you can store it behind the seat. How? Buy a round oak dowel and trim down the ends. You can also make these from a hardwood tree limb. Viney maple makes an excellent choice, as does oak. Cut the maple or oak limb so you have a sort of shepherd's crook on the bottom. Use that crook on opponents' ankles. When your club is over five feet long, you command respect. Using one requires two hands, however, and also requires some strength if you'll be using it like a pugil stick. Most martial artists teach this. Use yours as a walking stick so it's always with you.

44

CUTTING TOOLS
Many good fighting knives cost more than some handguns. Once you pull a knife, you escalate the battle to a lethal state. If the other party has a gun, your problem will be most severe. Though you need only one hand to cut with a knife, some knives require two hands to open or get ready. Avoid these.

Machetes. Long blades make them like swords. They're a little slow, although Blackjack crafts a super machete with a blade which gets thinner as it goes toward the tip. That makes it travel faster through the air at a target than you could believe. Also, you can use one for a much longer time without tiring. Practice will make you better. Get stainless steel. Some of the cheaper ones are high carbon steel and rust easily along the cutting edge, which makes a cutting edge dull. See *Everybody's Knife Bible.*

FOR OLDER FOLKS. READY ALWAYS
Use a cane if you have trouble walking. If you turn it around, you can hook any ankle and pull an assailant off balance. Pool-cue this into somebody's abdomen and the fight is generally yours. An umbrella does the same, and frequently the end is pointed so it penetrates better.

DEALING WITH CRIME---THE EN-LIGHTENING METHOD
Buy a solid, metal, (4-5) cell police-type flashlight. Batteries add weight to make a striking blow effective. You can make a criminal really see the light if you hit him with a five-cell steel flashlight. One goes under the seat of your car and is a great deterrent---just the sight of these things scare a lot of career criminals because of memorable police encounters. Techniques with this are the same as you would use with a stick. Turned sideways and held with two

hands, you can block all kinds of incoming blows. Raised over your head to strike, however, you'll be exposed and open to damage. Best strike with this light is pool-cue, but it also works well like a baseball bat at the knees. Only one hand operates this in striking mode. Therefore, use *something,* in your other hand, for example, spray gas.

CRIME CAN BE SHOCKING

You deliver 50,000 volts with some of the electrical shockers. But that's only if the battery is charged. Another problem, some people just don't respond to shock. Stun guns bring most criminals to a sagging heap on the floor, but there are problems. They sometimes have very little effect on a criminal, and you have to get in close to apply the electricity. That could be dangerous.

GETTING TO THE NITTY GRITTY

Sand or dirt. If your enemy is on the way in and you can grab a handful of sand or dirt, you can back-hand it into your opponent's face. The idea is to land it in the eyes, but you gain an advantage even if it only causes him to blink. Follow the sand with some decent kicks and blows---perhaps with your flashlight.

ROCK-A-BYE BABY

How's your arm? Can you throw with speed and accuracy? Don't forget rocks. It only takes a few of these to provide ammunition you can use effectively before your target ever gets close. This ammunition costs nothing, and practice is fun.

A confident stance with one of these weapons will often be enough to scare an attacker away. Most criminals don't fear jail; they fear bodily harm. When you have a weapon and a willingness to use it, your posture will be more erect, your stare steady and offensive, and your balanced body weight will indicate confidence. Any street fighter recognizes that these are signs of trouble. Therefore flashing any one of these weapons may be enough to avoid a struggle. Remember, you may have to fight; be prepared.

One important thing to know: All weapons, whether they be non-shooting or firearms, have a position in a hierarchy. Against a superior weapon, you'll have to make up the difference. How? With strength, speed, skill and/or determination. Baseball bats always do better than a rock in a sock. Knives are OK, but have no place in a gun fight.

Bare hands come in last. That's because weapons are extensions of your own ability to fight, and almost always enhance it upwards by several grades. Only in the movies will you see a karate guy disarm someone with an edged weapon. If _you_ want to try it, suture self.

Specialize. Find one weapon that matches your quickness, strength, and the range you need, and practice until you get good. Then practice more and often. Realize, however, that you and this weapon have limitations. Never use it to get into a squabble where you have an even chance of suffering severe physical damage. Staying secure from crime isn't about re-enforcing your pride; it's about keeping you alive and healthy.

When you add the price of medical rehabilitation for injury to the price of goods stolen after you get hurt, you'll understand right away---you're better off to let them have what they want instead of risking your corpus to protect it. But if you have to protect a loved one, do it with the confidence only a weapon can produce.

IMPROVISED WEAPONS

Most people become victims because they were unprepared. You may someday find yourself in a threatening situation when you're not armed. Therefore, it's a good idea to know how to use a variety of things you have around you as improvised weapons.

Incidentally, you can talk defense all you want, but take a lesson from football coaches: <u>The best defense is a good offense.</u> In today's society, offense isn't considered right, so talk "defense," but then know what it really is. If the need to defend arises, attack---ferociously.

SHREDDED GLASS

Grab a thick piece of cloth and break a window, then wrap the cloth around a piece of glass and slice with it. A small chunk of concrete or a rock in a belt will also do a good job. Military belts cinch all the way up and tighten down on concrete. If your belt is leather, punch some extra holes in near the buckle. Practice swinging so the return arc of the swing is not in line with your body.

CAR KEY IN YOUR FIST

Master locksmith Eric Smith from San Clemente told me that filing the flat sides of a key won't disturb its ability to open locks. Even better than filing your own keys, go to a Toyota dealer and buy a steel blank with the hard plastic cover on the handle. Sharpen the point with a file. Now--- make a fist. Put the key between your index and middle finger. Punch anything and the sharp key will penetrate an inch or so to cause severe pain, etc.

SODA CANS. TAKE TIME OUT TO GET READY

You'll need some preparation time for this one. Still, in what might develop into a tough situation, you can put this

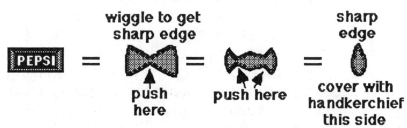

wiggle to get sharp edge

sharp edge

PEPSI = ⟐ = ⟐ = ◊

push here

push here

cover with handkerchief this side

together and be better prepared than you would be with nothing.

Crunch a soda can following the steps from left to right. When the can is completely crunched, you can use a fingernail clipper file to make the sharp edge even sharper. Cover the back side of the can with a handkerchief so it doesn't dig into your palm. Then rake it down the face of an attacker. Women: This will normally reduce sexual excitement for an unarmed rapist.

ROCK IN A SOCK

Take off your shoe, remove one sock, and put your shoe back on. It will feel funny. Drop a rock in your sock. Shorten your grip so you swing from the sock's heel. (Otherwise, it may swing around and hit you.) Use the newly weighted sock to hit your assailant over the head. Rough rocks will also work, but they often cut into the material.

Critical Advice: Weapons can be anything which lengthens or strengthens your defensive ability. They enable you to take on superior force---if you keep them. Most superior forces try to take them away. Don't strike once and wait around. Retract the weapon as quickly and forcefully as you hit with it. Then, never stand around and wait for your attacker to regain consciousness. Either strike again, or leave the scene immediately.

Naturally, respect the hierarchy of weapons. Never get into a battle with a weapon inferior to that of your adversary. If the other guy is carrying something that has more range, speed, power, control, target accuracy, and operational convenience, **don't engage!**

The choices in all conflict is fight or flight. Choose the former **only** when you know for certain you can prevail without getting injured or wounded. Otherwise, choose flight. Finally, if you can't run and he has better weapons--- choose life. Act as if you give up. Watch carefully for the first sign your assailant is relaxing. Now, **strike!**

VICTIM INSURANCE FOR CRIMINALS

Shouldn't it be mandatory for anyone who goes to jail to carry victim insurance or stay in jail? In almost every state in the union, auto insurance is mandatory. Lawmakers have devised several methods of enforcement. Uninsured drivers pay severe penalties.

If a driver can't drive without insurance because of the possibility of accident, then no convict should go free without insurance because of the high probability of his committing a new crime. Statistics show that convicted criminals are likely to commit new crimes, yet they need carry no victim insurance.

Chapter 4

TRAINING FOR DEFENSE / NON SHOOTERS

Most victims of criminal germs became victims because they never got ready to fight the battle. They were caught by surprise, didn't know what to do, were too terrified to think, and lost by default. Those who live through the experience explain their losses with phrases such as, ". . .right out in broad daylight;" or, . . "there was a whole gang of them;" or, "right in my own yard." Sad---but they could've won the battle with only a little preparation and training.

When you increase training, you lessen the chances of losing in criminal conflict. To be sure, in the event you're faced with a violent situation and you don't have access to a firearm, you can use a handy knife, club or other non-shooting weapon. But you need to practice so you'll be able to strike quickly with power. Often, you can turn a losing situation into a winning one with nothing more than a primitive weapon.

But don't go up against a firearm with a lesser weapon unless you have no choice. If the same thug pulls a gun on you while you only have a baseball bat, do nearly anything he tells you. But then, take advantage of any diversion that might occur. Watch for the smallest opportunity. Looking for anything you can get your hands on to use as a weapon—-anything. There's a good chance that your training and practice will carry the moment.

Training does important things for you. First, personal stress--- especially in a life-or-death situation---can block your ability to think clearly and quickly; sometimes you won't be able to think at all. Training helps to take you out of this paralysis. Second, to be quick and effective, you need to be able to perform by rote, like a robot. If you don't train, you don't develop any habit of action. Third, you have to pre-form a determined attitude of counter offense in order to overcome what the Los Angeles PD calls "lag time." It's normal for most good citizens to be appalled at the prospect of shooting, knifing, or beating someone with a club, but those actions may be required for survival. To succeed in war, you have to fight better than the enemy. If you have the slightest doubt about the animal mentality of the modern criminal, read a few crime reports.

ATTITUDE TRAINING
Every time you train with a weapon, you re-enforce your defensive attitude. Don't just stand there hitting a tree or fence post with your Bo. Imagine this to be real—-a life or death situation with a drug crazed moron who wants to hurt you. Strike accordingly! Avoid all the trouble you can. But if you can't avoid trouble, decide now to give the other side an opportunity to find out first hand if there really is life after death.

In line with keeping your attitude right, learn the concept of focus. Focus intensely on the part of the anatomy you want to attack. As defined by Sun Duk Sun, the 9th degree grand master of Tae Kwon Do, "focus" means you bring all of your strength, heart, mind, soul, and striking force to one point on your opponent's anatomy.

How does your conscience

RESULTS OF TRAINING FOR DEFENSE

Action by rote

Developed counter—offense attitude.

Trained muscle memory

PREPARED DEFENDER

Physical condition

Learn to block incoming

react to all of this? Let us help you. The anger and hatred the perp exhibits weren't caused by you. You'll feel as if you caused it. But the attitude is his—-and always will be. Those hateful sentiments were rooted in this germ long before you encountered him, and will still be there long after. You can rely on that, even though the jerk doesn't think so. He never gets a clue that the real problem is his alone.

To prepare for war, you do two types of training: a. You train physically with the non-shooting weapon of your choice. Make sure you can strike your target often with precision and strength. Set aside between one to four hours a month when you can work out with the weapon you've chosen. Don't try to become proficient with a Bo, a Tonfa, and your baseball bat. Choose one weapon, and half a dozen moves and strikes. What's the best time to practice with a weapon? After dark. That's when most criminals go to work. Also, you'll be less self conscious.

b. Train with your firearm at least on a monthly basis; you can't train too much. Don't merely go to a range, stand up sideways, and shoot. Use barricades; shoot and move; practice a lot at night. In the desert or woods, find an old car you can shoot at from various angles so you know how your particular rounds will penetrate. Shoot through wood as well. Caution: Bullet holes don't belong in anyone else's property. Bring your own wood to shooting practice. Don't ever shoot through an old, abandoned building without checking inside to see who's sleeping there first. Don't send out wild lead; make sure of your backstop.

DEFENSIVE SPRAY GAS. Work with a different bottle of spray so you learn to aim the real thing. Inspect the spray nozzle on your Mace can; then buy a similar spray can of window cleaner. Now, with the window cleaner, close your eyes, feel for the can, and try to spray ahead of you. If I get my wish, you sprayed window cleaner anywhere but the target. Here's the point: Modify your Mace spray can so you can use it at night. You need both to see the spray direction easily, and feel it. Some spray packages are designed to help you spray without seeing the can. Sabre CS gas mixed with red pepper, for example, sprays right out of the leather case.

If the can of Sabre Gas you bought will spray like a paint can, (in any direction unless you aim), it needs some modification. Pick up the can with your spraying hand. Mark the side of the can where your thumb will rest. Cut a piece of plastic off a plastic fork and use one of the super glues to stick it right where your thumb goes. This way, when your thumb is on the bump, you'll spray straight ahead. Place a similar bump on your practice can of window cleaner. Now you can practice with your eyes closed. With a little training, you'll be able to use Mace in the dark. We recommend that you train with your Mace in your weak (left?) hand so you can free up your strong hand for a second weapon. If you spray someone and they keep on coming toward you, you have a reasonable right to be in mortal fear, and therefore, to use more force. If you'll use a handgun in your right, practice spraying with your left. Once you know where it aims, spray the cleaner on a mirror or window in which you can see your own image. Spray your own reflection in the face; center on the nose. Make sure you go through the motions with your own can. Get proficient enough to unlock any safety device on your Mace can and spray quickly with only one hand.

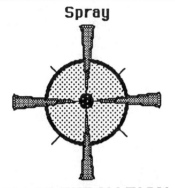

Spray

MACE THE NATION

While many commercial sprays are set up so you can shoot them by feel (at night) some of those same commercial sprays are illegal in some states. In California, for example, lawmakers made red pepper gas illegal, presumably because it did temporary damage to perpetrators. On the other hand, wasp killer, which probably does permanent damage, is legal, so carry that instead. Since wasp killers are really intended to kill wasps however (an activity done during daylight hours) you <u>must modify your can</u> so you can use it at night just by feeling it.

KEY CHAINS KEYED TO DEFENSE. Makiwara sticks aren't very useful unless you study karate and learn to snap with them. Many people install them on a key ring. If you do that, put a one ounce sinker on the ring also; then hold the handle to swing the sinker into your attackers head.

LONG RANGER. The Bo. You can learn to use one by watching a video. Practice on fence posts, trees, and tall shrubs. Naturally, you can pool-cue this a longer distance away than a short weapon will allow. But——<u>you gotta be quick</u>. (That's why you train.) Otherwise, they'll take it away from you. This weapon works well in the old, rifle-butt-stroke mode. If you make your own Bo from a tree limb, leave a hook on one (lower) end. That way, you increase its usability; you can hook the legs out from under any attacker before he gets too close. The Bo is also an excellent blocking weapon. Tapering the ends makes the Bo lighter; therefore, it will strike faster and harder. With green hardwood, bake it over an open fire; the heat will harden the wood like iron.

CUTTING TOOLS. Often, when people use a knife for defense, lag time gives the perp a good chance to take the weapon away from them. Severe problem! Don't buy a knife for defense unless you plan to spend the time and money to learn how to use it effectively. A rubber knife of the same size and shape makes a lot of sense for practice. One knife maker prominently into knives for weapons is Cold Steel. Another is our favorite for quality, Blackjack. The company's owner is a leading authority on edged weapon combat. To be effective with a knife, you really have to practice a lot. You'll need to develop speed, strength, stamina, and a lot of fortitude, because knife fighting is almost an intimate sport. Avoid bad judgement, fatal error and bad manners:

Never bring a knife to a gunfight.

MARTIAL ARTS
Karate-do means: The way of the empty hand. Weapons training makes you more effective because weapons extend and increase your defense capability. Learning a martial art is good because many martial art moves make your weapons work better, more effectively, faster, and safer (because you learn to strike in balance and not over-extend).

Martial arts training is extremely useful but it may trap you in the beginning, when you begin to feel your own power and think you're now invincible. Another problem, especially for women, is this: you have to let your attacker come in close (well inside three yards) before you can work your defensive magic.

But you should be attacking long before the germ gets that close. Also, the kind of martial arts most women choose to study is karate. It doesn't work well on a grappler, which is what most rapists and women abusers are. Once they grapple with you, they're too close to kick and the contest is often decided by pure strength and size.

Still, martial arts training offers multiple benefits. Any martial art will get you into better than average physical condition, which will lessen your chances of failing in other areas of defense. It will also increase your chances of winning in violent confrontations if your gun isn't with you. Knowing one or two thoroughly effective and disabling moves really well can make the difference between winning or dying. In a case where using a firearm creates an unacceptable level of risk to people you're trying to protect, having the ability, courage and confidence to attack without a firearm is a good idea. To use a knife or club as a primary defense weapon, you must take at least some martial arts training. If you don't understand the ways in which the body can be made to perform faster and with more applied

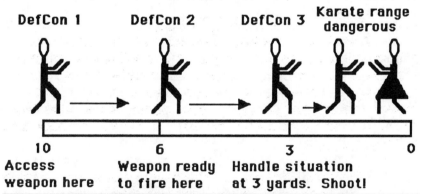

DefCon 1	DefCon 2	DefCon 3	Karate range dangerous
10	6	3	0
Access weapon here	Weapon ready to fire here	Handle situation at 3 yards. Shoot!	

DEFCON SYSTEM OF PREPARING FOR CONFLICT
The DefCon (**Defense Condition**) system keeps you from getting caught by surprise because you didn't pay attention to a potential problem early enough. Martial arts training tends to teach you to handle problems inside your three-yard limit. You're better off to address the problem at ten yards.

strength, you won't be able to use a weapon to its fullest advantage or you may lose it during combat. Also, you need to understand blocking and parrying, because in any fight, someone wants to hurt you. Martial arts helps you develop a fighting attitude.

Finally martial arts training is an excellent confidence builder. Confidence is important because that attitude shows in the way you walk (upright, shoulders back, with purpose) and in your tone of voice. Don't worry about what kind of martial art to pursue. You'll get something from just about any study you take.

Your idea may be to take only one short lesson in how to come out a winner in hand-to-hand combat. But, karate instructors have spent years studying their own disciplines. (That's the only way to get a black belt in anything.) If you go to any martial arts class, you'll be studying their martial art. Just make sure the class has one vital element: sparring. Listen to Bruce Lee in a line from *Enter the Dragon.* He says, "Boards do not hit back." If you don't get a chance to face off with other opponents and spar (no contact is required), you aren't training for combat; you're just learning motions to punch holes in the air.

> Most criminals are grapplers when they fight. When they get in too close to you like this, karate doesn't work as well as judo, jujitsu, or aikido.

```
CLOSE RANGE COMBAT
WHERE STRENGTH AND SIZE
PLAY A BIG PART IN CONTEST
```

Grappling Range
Too close for Karate

Get a physical checkup if you have any doubts about your condition. Martial arts training can be very strenuous activity. So is active fighting during an attack. If you learn the arts but then fall out of practice and condition, a hard fight will just about do you in.

When all is said and done, you need to know what the limitations of your ability are. Even if you have a sixth degree black belt, be aware of two things: A. Mental preparation is important; it goes hand in hand with physical ability. You simply have to be ready to attack savagely. A good "street fighter" who is ready and willing to do battle can overcome any karate expert who is not mentally set. B. Firearms are king. The only time a firearm loses to a club or clever karate move is in the movies. If someone else has the firearm and you have a black belt and a Bo, back down, run away, or give up your wallet. Nobody's tougher than a bullet.

WHY BUILD MORE PRISONS IN THE U.S?

Where does it say that after committing a crime, the US owes a criminal a comfortable free ride in a prison in American territory? Prisons are overcrowded; early releases are flooding society with human sewage before treatment. Federal penitentiaries are sought-after places for criminals to do time.

Bond issues for prisons spend taxes in advance which may be needed for future problems such as natural disasters, failure of government-insured businesses like savings and loans, or a war.

Solution: contract with foreign governments in Third World countries to take care of our prisoners on a lease basis. Lease facilities in South Korea, Mexico, or Siberia for a fraction of the cost, about $6 per day per prisoner. Problems with visitation? Establish a tele-video communications network.

MARTIAL TO CIVIL LAW SLIDE ON RIGHTS

Who should get more rights—criminals, or the citizens they oppress?   Is our civil, as opposed to martial, law system working to provide us with a safe environment in which to pursue our inalienable rights? If not, why not martial law? Too stringent?

Then how about a law system in between the extremes of martial and civil? If the function of a law system is to provide a safe atmosphere for citizens, why not control civil rights on a scale?   Let's modify civil law to become increasingly martial as crime increases in a given area.   Otherwise, criminals operate under an umbrella of protection from our law, causing criminal anarchy to be the real rule in places such as Washington D.C. New York, and South Central L.A.

ELECTRONIC DATA ADMISSABLE IN PROSECUTION

Wolf ears and long distance zoom cameras used by casual citizens can now easily record drug deals by crack dealers, murders, robberies, and various assaults as they did for Rodney King.

In the military intelligence business, anything broadcast over the airwaves is free and usable information. Should something out of a criminals mouth be private when we think we're waging a war on crime? We need new laws to make such information automatically public domain.   Therefore, it will be admissible as evidence in criminal trials. Second, we need to pay a reward for the information. It will turn thousands of citizens into private eyes, convict huge numbers of crack and other drug dealers, and be far cheaper than paying police salaries.

COURT DECREE: DESIGNATED ENEMY OF UNITED STATES

After one final attack on society, the straw that breaks us, why not judiciously designate the person a designated enemy of the United States, which would give anyone the perfect right to defend against him without fear of prosecution, cops included. Once any criminal has been designated an enemy, then no charges of any kind could have been brought up against the police officers who beat and arrested him. Moreover that criminal would long ago have accumulated enough points to lose his citizen's standing to sue. How can a down and dirty, repeat, one man crime wave offender retain any rights in this country?

"I certainly don't wish to spend whatever remaining time the Lord allows me on earth in the company of jailed convicts. But if the choice is being buried or being jailed, I'll accept jailed." Craig Huber

Chapter 5

HOW TO DEFEND YOURSELF IN AND AROUND WHERE YOU LIVE

Preparation is your greatest friend. When trouble comes, you probably won't be able to think. During a battle, the fight-or-flight syndrome takes over, and the brain (and maybe the rest of your body) simply leaves. So, the necessary moves and actions you make in the midst of battle have to be done by developed instinct and habit. You can't think about it—-you won't be able to.

Without preparation, most violent confrontations in your home will cause you to panic, whereupon you lose. We think so many people panic during invasion of their home or vehicle because both places are thought of as safe spaces. Intrusion into that space overloads sensitivity and therefore can cause panic. **Panic**, remember, is your greatest enemy in any defense situation.

PUTTING YOUR DEFENSE PLAN INTO EFFECT
After committing to your plan of defense, create safety in your home. Consider all the possibilities you may need to defend against, then plan to handle them. Timing counts. When a "defensive" situation arises it's almost always too late to think about how to deal with it. It's going to rain crime pretty soon; get your umbrella ready. First, do those things which don't require outside help or new equipment purchases. Don't wait for all the parts to come together. You may not have time. Do what you can immediately.

How about your defense plan? Does the whole family know about it? Do children know about the changes in your home and life style to accommodate your plan? Are your doors and windows secure? Does your defense plan include firearms? Is your weapon with you at home and loaded with the correct ammunition? Can you get to it right away in an emergency? Choose a sanctuary or safe room. Get it ready. Make a decision about your last line of defense. Your safe room entrance should allow you to cover all other sleeping area entrances.

To be prepared at all times, provide yourself with early warnings. Listen carefully to the sounds your house already makes. Squeaky doors or loose floorboards can be blessings and should be left to squeak if they provide information. Add sound effects to your home's surroundings. Gravel beds just outside your downstairs windows make it so nobody can step there without crunching. In season, dry leaves raked below windows do the same. Small dogs generally sleep in your bedroom; they growl slightly when they hear something human ears can't detect. The result: you're awake and ready long before someone breaks into your home, but the perpetrator never heard the rumbling warning your dog gave you.

TACTICAL HOUSE LIGHTING
Don't set up a pattern with your interior house lighting. If you only leave outside lights on at night when you're away, professional criminals who pattern victims have a perfect signal telling them when your house is vacant. Vary your activities as much as possible. Buy a few timer switches which turn inside lights on and off for you. Use automatic sensor-switch outdoor floodlighting.

EMERGENCY: HOUSE BURGLARY
You get a call; there's a severe emergency. You jump in the car, race to the hospital, and no emergency. When you get home, everything's gone.

Don't leave your home and family unguarded. If your loved one is already in the hospital, getting there five minutes later is going to make very little difference. Always check emergency calls. With a call-verifier gadget on your phone which you can now purchase from many telephone supply outlets, note the number from which the call originates. Otherwise, ask for the name and phone number of the caller and find out who (doctor, police officer, etc.) and where, they are. Call the number right back to verify and check the phone number against the supposed location.

WHEN SOMEONE COMES TO YOUR DOOR
Always identify law enforcement personnel by ID card as well as badge. Familiarize yourself with the ID cards of police, sheriffs, and federal law enforcement agencies. The above goes double for anyone not in uniform. Check them out before admitting them. Some men now come to the door in a public utility uniform. They'll give you a number, but it's really a pay phone answered by an accomplice who says, "Utilities."

Post your front door: No solicitors. Never let any stranger into your home without an appointment. Likewise, never admit strangers with emergencies, even with an apparent injury. It's like picking up hitch hikers. You can do them a favor; i.e. take a number and make a phone call for them. While doing that, don't let them in or leave your door unlocked. They may follow you; once they're inside . . .

ON THE PHONE
Don't accept cold sales calls. Even if they're selling something you really want, don't go for it. Some companies will ship COD after the phone call whether or not you bought

---

Note: Where I might give up my life for my family or a close friend, I won't do that to protect things. I will let my possessions go as long as I am <u>positive</u> that by doing so I'm reducing the risk of injury or death. Of course, you may not be reducing risk by letting someone rob you. It's a judgment call.   *Craig*

---

anything. Others will sell several items, charge the correct COD amount, and be long gone when you discover something you paid for wasn't packed in the box.

Of course, be very careful about giving personal information over the phone. Questions about income, finances or personal wealth get no answer. All inquiries from private investigators should get a hang up. Most investigators work for attorneys. They'll either sue you or drag you into a case as a witness with a subpoena.

In addition to that, here's what **not** to do: Leave a recording on your phone answering machine that goes,
a.   "Hi, we're out of town for the next two weeks."
b.   "You have reached the Mulberries at 6224 Rip-off St."
c.   "You have reached 624-4567 at 2437 Haven Rd."
d.   "I sleep during the day, so I'll answer your call later."
e.   "We're probably out fishing."
f.   "If it's you, Sally, we left a key under the mat."

To the wrong person, here's how those messages translate: **a.** You have two weeks before anybody will know you broke in. **b.** Drive to this house and call from your car phone. If no one answers again, break in. **c.** Phone number with house address. You can clear it for break-in later. **d.** Rapists delight for working women. Burglars delight at night. **e.** Check to see if the boat is gone too; then break in. **f.** My elevator doesn't go all the way to the top.

DEALING WITH NUISANCE, OBSCENE, OR THREATENING PHONE CALLS

HANG UP! Don't talk to the callers, don't threaten them or ask anything. Just hang up and call the operator, then police. Act immediately after the first call. Buy a call identifier. Even with out one, you can pretend. "I have the number you're calling from on my call verifier. Stay there while I call the police." That should take care of the problem.

It's best not to list your number in the directory. If you do, however, don't use your full name. As we all know, most single women who list in the directory use a first initial only. It was a way to avoid obscene calls until perverts figured it out and started dialing first initial names. <u>Single men!</u> You can do a big favor for hundreds of harassed women. If you list your phone, don't use your full first name——only your first initial. That way, all the hot breath callers won't be able to pick women out of the phone book by first initial only. I thank you, my sister thanks you, and your next date will think you're kind and considerate.

LIKE HOWARD HUGHES---MAINTAIN PRIVACY
Many divorcees wish not to be discovered or disturbed by an ex-spouse. Have your phone issued to a John or Jane Doe. Don't list it publicly, and give it out only to trusted friends.

DEFENDING YOURSELF AT HOME
Think like a criminal while preparing your defense. React like a soldier while carrying it out. The greatest enemy in any stress situation is panic. The greatest cures for panic are preparation and training. To develop an effective plan, first assess the various threats you're likely to face, both at home and on the street. How can you do this? The military calls the gathering of information about the situation, terrain around us, the enemy, his strengths, and his methods of operation intelligence. Without all this intelligence, you may very well make some bad decisions.

WHAT DO YOU NEED TO KNOW?
Is your neighborhood attractive to house burglars? Why? Can the situation be changed or improved? Is there a convicted sex offender living in the immediate area? Is the incidence of assault, robbery, or rape on the increase or decrease? These are questions you need answers to before you can begin your defense planning. Other questions are important, too. Is your neighborhood near a major civil disturbance site? Are you close to a state fair ground or carnival site? Is a convention center or high rent business

district close by? Is your neighborhood located near a rock concert site? All of these factors can elevate the threat level in an area because of the transients they attract.

Several sources will tell you about any area? Of course, check the yellow pages. Adult movies and pawnshops are normally located in areas you should avoid at night. Cross that area out on your map. In the library, check the local paper's "police blotter" or "crime corner" column. If the paper is on microfiche, it's easy to read how things have gone for the last few months. For everyone, male or female, the best, low-down gossip is always obtainable at the local hair salon. Book an appointment, get a shampoo and cut, and spend some time listening to your hair stylist or manicurist. They know enough about the neighborhood to earn a living as local gossip columnists. Individual police officers may be a valuable source of information. They can tell you about the level and kinds of crime in a neighborhood.

Your future neighbors can be a great source of local intelligence. Visit them and ask a few questions about what goes on in the area. A quick trip around the neighborhood will tell you a lot, too. Look and listen. Are the homes generally in a good state of repair? Is the greenery trimmed, trash picked up? A neighborhood allowed to deteriorate is often an indication of trouble. Do many of the homes have alarm systems? Are there junked cars in the yards? Are adult males loitering during working hours? Do you hear sounds of domestic unrest? How do older children react to you? Are they respectful, or surly? Are young children open and friendly—-or fearful and remote? Tatoos of similar kinds, kids hanging around together doing nothing, and cars doctored up to ride low are signs of rebellion and gang membership. Maybe you ought to live elsewhere.

Two final death signs: Graffiti and burglar bars over windows. If you see either of these, you know gangs are within walking distance. Graffiti spray painting on walls is the same thing your dog does on bushes. The only thing worse than graffiti is graffiti crossed out or overwritten. You'll see one sign crossed out with a "no" next to it, and a rival gang sign over that with the word "si" next to it. That spells "disrespectful challenge," and it means the locals will soon make stronger statements punctuated by periods---of gunfire. The home you're considering buying may not be air conditioned, but we can guarantee it'll soon be ventilated.

REAL ESTATE---LOCATION, LOCATION

With security in mind, don't choose a home simply for a view, the house, the acreage or the school zone. What makes a neighborhood good or bad has only to do with the people who live there and the frequent passers-by. Before you buy, spend a lot of time in the neighborhood. Walk around and talk to people. Many neighborhoods change radically after dark---but most homes are shown by agents during the day only. Would you be safe taking a walk near this home after sundown? Many people live under the constant fear of crime in American neighborhoods.

Professional thieves don't just drive into a neighborhood at random and start robbing houses. They may "case" an area for days before making a move. It makes sense for you to use this same technique and patience when choosing a home. Learn what a burglar looks for. Then buy the opposite.

Think about this. The enemy is out there, and they're looking for plunder. You want your house to be a less attractive target than other houses. If a neighborhood defense team is active, the whole area will be a less attractive target. If the enemy is going to target a house, an individual, or victim, he will most often choose the target easiest to hit. Anything you can do to make the criminal think this house or person is more difficult will be a step in the right direction. You can't eliminate risk; you merely reduce it. Load the odds in your favor.

Ask a local agent what auto insurance will cost if you buy in a certain area. In some suburbs, auto insurance premiums are out of sight unless a theft exclusion is written in the policy. Insurance rates in Santa Barbara (70 miles North) cost about half of the L.A. rates. Insurance companies can also tell you about house burglaries. Compare premiums for home content insurance. Higher premiums for comparable coverage indicate a higher level of risk.

Is your house interior visible from the street? Privacy sheer curtains allow you to see out, but keep you invisible as long as there is more light outside. Are all the doors and ground floor windows clear of shielding shrubs or fencing? Are there areas from which your home can be watched without the watcher being seen and attracting attention? Trim your trees to provide 3-4 feet of clearance from the lowest branch to the ground. You don't want to provide a shield for burglars to hide behind while they work to get past your doors and windows. Neither do you want to provide an ambush site for a personal attack. In addition, ask these questions: Does your house look richer or easier to break into? Can your house be approached from more than one direction by someone in a vehicle? Can a vehicle be parked near your home and not be visible to your neighbors or from a passing patrol?

Think about this: How would you get into your house if you locked yourself out? Can you make your home much less accessible to an intruder and still allow for emergency entry by yourself? What can you do for yourself and for what will you need outside help? Can you count on yourself to deal with most confrontations or should you consider ways to summon help? Let security take priority over convenience or comfort. The next time you consider buying a new toy for your house, think first whether or not you can protect it.

Develop your security plan around your own abilities. Do you have previous firearms experience? Do you have religious convictions which would cause you to hesitate in a defense situation? Be realistic as you assess your strengths and weaknesses. Are you strong enough, equipped to fight, and well enough trained? Can you run? Could you get yourself in condition? Can you correct the problems you find in and around your home? Will the cost be prohibitive? If so, is a move possible?

Start your home defense planning with pen and paper. Start a quarter mile from your home and work your way back home in rough circles. An active neighborhood defense team will help a lot because other members widen your sphere of defense. Walk around; make notes. You miss too much if you drive.

FOR SUPER SECURITY---A NEIGHBORHOOD DEFENSE TEAM

Nobody can rob you if they can't even get into the neighborhood. Why fight crime alone? You can form a team just like a Green Beret Team and benefit from specialists who will help make your neighborhood invincible. They key is to choose good people of high character. Under the team leader, specialties are: Medic, Communications, Construction engineer, Animal technician, Firearms, Supply, and Fire Suppression.

All work at increasing skill levels in each specialty. Medic answers health care emergencies. Communications monitors police scanner, has independent commo net to members' homes, and links with foot and auto patrols. Construction specializes in fortifications for individual homes and street barricades. Animal technician trains defense dogs and works with owners. Firearms helps acquire weapons and teaches marksmanship. Supply does procurement for team tools and standard issue. Fire suppression maintains and stores all fire fighting equipment and inspects for fire safety.

Much more than neighborhood watch, team families patrol with binoculars and radios to stay in touch with communications. Cars not belonging in the neighborhood are scrutinized.

The team interacts and trains together and prepares for all kinds of criminal invasions. More? Fourteen pages: $1 + postage.

SETTING GOALS

As in many things, the simplest plan is often best. Set defense goals and be specific. Think, "I want to reduce the risk of having my home burglarized, having my children molested, having a violent confrontation in or near my home, or having my car stolen, broken into, or vandalized. I want to increase my chances of coming out the winner in any confrontation I can't avoid."

A useful set of goals might read like this:

To develop a defense plan for both my family and our home.

To reduce the risks of becoming a victim of violence.

To reduce the risks of being a victim of thieves or burglars.

To make my home less attractive to criminals.

To increase my chances of winning any violent confrontation I can't avoid.

Prepare to do **whatever is necessary** to accomplish your goals. Be advised: You may have to kill. Be sure you're prepared to do that or your defense plan could become useless. Worse, it could turn a bad situation into a lethal situation with an outcome exactly opposite of your plan. If you pick up a weapon and think you can get by with bluffing, think again. The criminal has lived and survived on the streets for years. In a New York minute, they can discern the difference between your fear and your very real threat of force.

PRACTICE YOUR PLAN. AVOID ALL THE TROUBLE YOU POSSIBLY CAN.

Plan to avoid a violent personal confrontation whenever possible, but prepare to deal with any confrontation you can't avoid, and win it—-decisively!

IF YOU ALREADY HAVE THE RIGHT, WHY A LICENSE?

Why is a license required for you to exercise your constitutional right to bear arms? Can a licensing entity deprive you of a right without due process? Could congress simply raise taxes on guns and ammunition? If they do, will only rich people (including drug dealers) or thieves, acquire guns?

Chapter 6

HOW TO DEFEND VEHICLES
AGAINST THEFT AND CARJACKING.
THE FASTEST GROWING CRIME—-CARJACKING

More and more crime occurs to people while in and around vehicles. Rental car agencies now charge as much as $17 per day for insurance, a large part of which is for theft.

Carjacking is a crime in which the enemy gets your car, your purse, and all the property you keep in your car. *USA TODAY* wrote in October, 1992 that carjacking has become a rite of passage for gang members. The germs steal your car, then drive it around for a few days to show off. Of course, some do it for money. In a chop shop, parts off your car are worth four times the value of the vehicle.

LOSING YOUR CAR WHILE DRIVING IT

Here's one way: You stop at a traffic light. Two germs team up. One steps off the curb in front of your car just as the light turns yellow. The other comes up from behind. With his back turned to traffic behind you, he taps on your window with a pistol and orders you out of the car. You get out quickly and run for your life. He jumps in and drives off. You think you should call for police to report your car stolen, but you really need to send the police to your home. Why? Attached to your car keys are your home keys, and your auto registration in the glove compartment carries your home address. He may go there next. Quick; call home! Warn your family!

Take precautions against carjacking. For starters, detach your car keys from your house keys. Use a post office box mailing address on your auto registration. Memorize your license number.

Improve your rear vision. Don't drive a car without two side view mirrors. It's a good idea to install a multi-window rear view mirror so you can see all your blind spots. If someone steps off the curb in front of you to block your escape, drive ahead slowly. The LAPD advises, "You're not driving your vehicle over someone if they have a chance to get out of the way." Once you see a move toward a weapon, step on the gas and go. Don't idle up, right behind someone's bumper, save some maneuvering space between you and the car ahead, say, a car length. Practice that. You need to develop the habit.

ROOM AT STOPLIGHT
TO ESCAPE FROM CARJACKING

On occasion, someone steals a police car and rapes women who pull over in a dark area after the perp flashes red lights. Any doubts? Don't stop in a dark area; drive slowly ahead to a well lit, crowded area.

You're most vulnerable to attack just as you get into, or out of, your car. That's when the germs like to hold you up at gun point, which can happen in a variety of circumstances. Perhaps they follow you out of a shopping mall. As you get to the car, they attack. Rest stops and gas stations are also ambush places where the germs attack. Chances of being robbed go up in places such as poorly lit parking lots after hours and underground parking garages where you have to venture alone.

Perps know your back is turned while you're opening your door. You can fix that. 1. Tint your side windows and keep them clean so you can use them as a mirror. 2. Check your perimeter before you approach your car. 3. Don't look at your door lock. Stand back at arms length and scan the reflections in your car door windows. Look for movement. Soften your focus; don't stare at one spot on your window, but try and see the whole window at once. Thus, you'll be able to see anything on both sides of your reflected body.

Some of the most terrible crimes occur when someone follows the victim home. If they get you in the driveway, they get you, your house keys, five minutes of frantic shopping in your house, and your car. That's quite a rite of passage. To prevent this, we think the **rule of four turns** is best. From now on as you drive home, identify the car behind you. During the day you can observe the make, model, and occupants. During the night, you have to rely on street lights or close examination of the headlight-parking light configuration on the car behind you. Check to see if maybe one is out of adjustment with the other. How wide set are the lights in the car? Silhouette the occupants in front of back lighting and memorize the pattern; take notice of hats, hair, head heights, etc.

Now—-make four right turns. If the same car is behind you when you come back

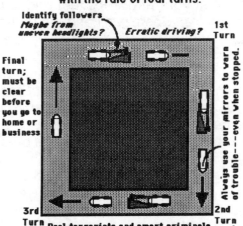

CARJACKING

How to give followers the slip with the rule of four turns.

Identify followers. Maybe from uneven headlights? Erratic driving? 1st Turn

Final turn; must be clear before you go to home or business

Always use your mirrors to warn of trouble---even when stopped.

3rd Turn

2nd Turn

Real terrorists and smart criminals know they've been made after this turn. Once they know you're on to them, they'll attack. Watch out!

out on your original route, you have a problem. Drive to a police station, a highway patrol office, or the busiest gas station you know. But, **don't** drive home. Incidentally, besides checking to see who is following you, make a habit of taking a quick look in the back seat before you climb into the car so you don't get in with a stowaway germ.

The germs also have a clever way of getting you out of your car while you're driving in traffic. They bump into you from behind. Knowing it's not your fault and being the good citizen you are, you step out right away to exchange insurance information. The advice on what to do in this situation has been changed. Now you drive slowly and in orderly fashion to a crowded gas station. Then step out. Otherwise, you'll step out into a crime as the driver who bumped into you or his accomplice deliberately jumps into your vehicle and drives away. One more caution: Don't let anybody come up to clean your windshield. If someone approaches with a spray bottle and towel, turn your windshield wipers on and command him to keep away.

When out of your car and someone pulls a gun on you, hit the deck and roll under a car. Once there, you can shoot at your attacker's feet and legs without taking serious return fire. Score a hit and the rest of his body will appear in your sights.

If you don't have a weapon and you're not prepared to shoot, Listen to the words of the LAPD: "Don't give up your privacy." Don't get into any car at gun point or allow some thug to get into your car. If a perp tries to force you into a car, just faint, go limp; become deadweight.

It's hard to know where the next ambush will be or the form it will take. During one ten-day period in Oakland, California, 15 victims were beaten, shot and robbed at the corner of 26th Street and Treat, a government project housing area. How? The oil can caper. The germs poured oil on the road so cars spun out; then they attacked.

Also new and becoming popular is this: The germ goes into a restaurant or store and tells management, "Arizona License # DPJ-378, a tan, 92 Mercedes left the headlights on." Remedy: Think, "did I really leave my lights on?" Don't get up; it's an ambush. The germs are out in the parking lot---waiting for you. At gun point, they take your keys, then drive off in your Mercedes. <u>Stores</u>, quit broadcasting unless you confirm. One more: A thug walks into a school and takes keys at gun point from a teacher during class. How? Teacher's shiny new car was parked in <u>a spot with her name on it.</u>

Just as some kinds of vehicles attract more criminals than others, so do some drivers. High-ticket foreign sports cars offer the most tempting targets. If you buy one of these, ask the dealer if it also comes with a high-ticket pistol. Female drivers attract more criminals than males do. They're thought of as weaker and easier victims. Also, the possibility of rape appeals to criminals. Carjackers prefer single occupants. unless the passenger is a child, in which case, they often threaten the child's life if you don't comply with their demands. Don't take these threats lightly. If they threaten you and don't follow through, they lose peer acceptance.

Huber's primary vehicle is a pickup truck. He had an auxiliary gas tank installed to extend his cruising range to over 500 miles. He makes a point of keeping the spare tank full. If you go the pickup route, consider a lift kit and big tires. Southland Corp. cut robberies in its 7-11 stores by raising the cash registers so robbers couldn't see the loot. In a perpetrator's mind, bigger trucks with tinted windows make vehicle robbery a lot more risky.

PURCHASING CONSIDERATIONS
The average person probably won't make defense from crime a number one priority when choosing a vehicle.

Regardless of the kind of car you buy, it will be safer with certain options: Think security. Consider power windows and power door locks. Power steering and anti-lock brakes give you an advantage when maneuvering defensively. Don't buy a car with a trunk opener down on the floor by the driver. Those levers attract window-busters, who then have only to lift the lever to get inside your trunk. Thus: you have no theft-secure place in the whole car to store anything.

Get a sturdy, heavy-duty vehicle with plenty of carrying capacity and a large fuel tank. You may have to evacuate your home during a civil disorder or natural disaster. Can you transport your whole family and the items you'll need for survival and comfort?

Along with all of the above, there are lots of things you can do to make your car safer and more theft proof. First, consider car burglary. Somebody wants your stereo, CB, tires, wheels, etc. Defense: Leave nothing visible. Remember, <u>most theft occurs as opportunity presents itself</u>. Never think your car is safe. Keep your car's interior sterile of things to steal, even while under way. Mount your CB under the seat or in a compartment overhead.

How about car theft itself? A locking device (like the Club) across your steering wheel helps, but you have to place it so the key inserts from the dash board side. Don't put the lock on your steering wheel with the lock pointing at the driver's seat. Otherwise, a car thief who just drilled the lock on your car door can use the same drill on the club.

A fuel shutoff valve prevents the car thief from driving far away. Special switches and alarms are also good. We've examined both the *Clifford and Viper Alarm* systems and

> They can't steal a car they can't start. Cut the eraser off the end of a wooden pencil. Pull the coil wire and push the eraser down in the hole, then replace the wire. That will block the electricity flow into the distributor; only a smart mechanic can start the car.

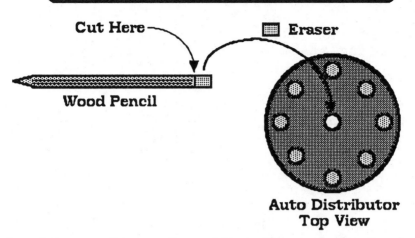

Can't Start \ Can't Steal

Cut Here

Eraser

Wood Pencil

**Auto Distributor
Top View**

found them to be excellent. Most will sound off only after your vehicle is disturbed by severe motion.

Keep your vehicle in first-class running condition. If your car breaks down, you may get robbed. At a minimum, make sure your tires are in good shape, all the belts are sound and the fluid levels are up to par. Have your vehicle checked regularly and perform the recommended oil changes, lubrication, and regular tune ups. We think the American Automobile Association is a great bargain. You can call for help on your cellular if your car breaks down.

AVOID SOLITARY CONFINEMENT
Without any communication to the outside world, you're an isolated prisoner when you drive. At least carry a sign for your window which says, "CALL POLICE." Better yet, install a CB radio and learn to use it. Channel nine (REACT) is often manned by base station operators who offer help and directions. Truckers routinely hang out on channel 17 & 19. You can learn to use a CB radio easily, and thereafter, help is only a push button away. Be careful though; anything you send over the airwaves could reach

the wrong ears. If you give your location over the radio, use direction, highway number, and closest mile marker (police procedure). One good place to install your CB is under your seat if you have room. Thieves normally don't steal what they can't see. Another is in the packaged ceiling kits you can get from automotive and RV mail order houses.

Install a cellular phone in your vehicle so you can call if someone starts hassling you on the road. Dial 911 and leave it in your phone, so you need only push one button to call for help quickly. Besides your cellular, use a police and emergency scanning unit in your car. Information you get over that radio let's you avoid bank robberies in progress, bad traffic accidents, and severe fires; plus, you get the latest news on new crime. In the event of trouble, don't leave your vehicle. If you don't have a cellular phone, summon help in the event of mechanical failure with a sign in the window, "HELP. CALL POLICE.

HIDE: DON'T LET THEM SEE YOU
Tint your car's windows. Your local dealer knows how dark you can go legally. I prefer a bit darker. What you want is a window which hides you and your loved ones from easy observation by criminals. Some random violence never happens because the perpetrator is unsure of his victim's capability for retaliation. Along with that line of reasoning, don't drive alone; get a mannequin or large doll for the passenger seat. Even a rubber mask from a costume store to put over your head rest will give the appearance of another passenger, especially with tinting.

Would you like yours darker than the law allows. Get a note from your dermatologist about the sun sensitivity of your skin. After tinting, be careful and courteous if stopped by police. Drive to a well lighted area, (they like that because it helps them see better) turn on your dome lights. Open both windows.

W h e t h e r walking or driving, getting lost can create a situation in which you become a victim. Install a GuideTech compass in your car to help you choose alternate routes. Also, in *Great Livin' in Grubby Times,* we spent pages teaching you how to modify your car for survival. One good idea: Install kevlar inside your door panels to make them bullet resistant.

PREVENTING CARJACKING

DRIVE AROUND GAS STATION IN A CIRCLE TO CHECK FOR BUMS AND GANGS BEHIND

DRIVING STRATEGY

Women, especially, should drive with a LIFO companion. LIFO means Last In, First Out, and that's how your passenger boards the vehicle. Men, quit driving. Let your wives drive; you ride shotgun. You can easily equip your car with a variety of pastime devices, including TV, stereo, Bible, or games to help pass the time while waiting. If you possibly can, go everywhere in pairs. Carry some kind of weapon with you always. If you don't want to shoot in a crowded mall, at least carry spray gas.

Carjacking from gas stations is also popular. I guess it beats robbing the station for $200. If you drive into a station at night, drive around behind it before you stop at the pumps. Drive into a parking lot or a gas station the same way a military patrol would come into an operational area. This is routine. Scouts set up a perimeter. In this case, the man is the scout, and the perimeter is the area around the car. The man gets out of the car while the engine is still running and checks things out. If he comes under attack, he can either dive back into the car or return fire as the driver gets away. But the driver doesn't travel very far. She has options. She can call for help, raise hell with the car horn and lights, play bumper cars with perpetrators on foot, or get far enough away and open fire with a long range weapon (rifle).

RENTAL CARS SEND A DANGEROUS SIGNAL TO KILLERS

Especially in Florida, where gun permits now have created an armed citizenry, criminals like to prey on tourists (no permit; no shoot back) and the license plates (from Manatee County) send a message: "Hit me; I'm a foreigner."

Cure: Camouflage. Bumper stickers from the airport gift shop show you to be a supporter of a local sports team. Of course, remove all rental stickers, including the bar code and small decal on the windshield.

Don't pull over and stop just because someone signals to you on a highway. One of the new ruses to maneuver you into a position where you can be attacked goes like this: They roll down their window on the highway, or signal to you frantically to pull over because your back wheel is rolling frontwards, or whatever. When you pull over, they pull up behind you as if to help, but they help themselves---to your car and person.

Another clever trick: The germs get a girlfriend with a baby to pull over to the side of the road and put the hood up. When you get out of your car to help, the perps come out of the bushes. Good Samaritans are now at risk.

SURVIVAL KIT FOR VEHICLES

Purchase a container for extra things you need in your car. A plastic, seal-tight box is inexpensive. Airtight food containers are my favorite because they are just the right size and waterproof. Fill the box with survival goodies. A pair of binoculars in your car enables you to read and record license numbers plus analyze a situation from a safe distance away.

Once you have a container or two, use bags to separate the things you need to store. Old shaving kit bags hold tools. Nylon zipper bags (fanny packs) hold material you might take with you on a hike. Below is a partial list of some things you might want with you.

Personal survival.
Drinking water. One gallon per passenger. Think also about your radiator.
Food. Make sure what you take won't spoil. Dried fruits, nuts, and seeds in a sealable container will work. Buy a few pounds of trail mix and replace it once in a while.
Clothes. Old boots are great. You can always get a few extra miles out of them, and you won't have to break them in during your emergency. You normally wear shoes in your car but, if your car breaks down, you may find yourself walking a long distance over rough terrain, so you'll need boots. In cold weather, it's absolutely essential to carry an MPI™ space blanket. They conserve 80% of your body heat and cost less than $15—-good insurance. These space blankets will also save you from frying in desert heat. Make a tarp out of them with the silver side up and crawl into the shade underneath.

Buy a First Aid kit and put it in a waterproof bag. Make sure your kit includes an air splint. They don't cost a lot, but most severe wrecks in vehicles require these. Training for first aid is best done by taking a red cross class.

Put a roll of quarters for emergencies and install them on the outside of your air filter in the air cleaner under your hood. You can keep spare keys there also unless your hood latch is inside the car. In that event, you have to hide a key outside the car, but only the one which opens the doors. Lose your keys? The Hide-a-key gets you into the car. The hood latch gets you to the ignition key so you can drive home.

Vehicle survival.

Fluids. Your car needs transmission fluid, (for emergencies, will work in engine also) motor oil, and coolant (water). Aluma-seal comes in a small package a little larger than a roll of quarters. If you get a hole in your radiator, you can pour the seal in when the water is hot and the seal will plug the leaks.

Spare parts. Belts, hoses, worm drive hose clamps, bulbs, seal beams, old rotor, and a couple old spark plugs. Just save the old ones when you install new. Buying new ones and leaving them in your trunk can cause this problem: You suffer an emergency or enemy attack. To avoid the problem, you strain your vehicle to the max at high speed or on rough ground. A radiator hose or water pump belt gives out. You hurry to install the new one, but it's the wrong size! Put new ones on the car; old ones in the trunk.

Tools. Again, old ones. Just make sure to use them before you toss them in the trunk. Don't buy new junkers. Garage sale it and put together a set of good old (perhaps Craftsman?) tools you can rely on. Many new, cheap import tools fail with just one use. Try 4 screw drivers, (two Phillips), three pliers (needle, water pump, and regular) 3/8th's drive socket set, open end/box end wrenches, 2 crescent wrenches, and some hammers. You may need to pound a fender away from a tire so you can drive away. Add a stainless, lock-back folding knife which you can open with one hand. The factory keeps them razor sharp for you.

Also, add a pre-packed roadside trouble kit which contains flares, jumper cables and a flashlight. Don't forget tow rope and perhaps a used come-along (about $10).

Practice with your car's jack to make sure you're familiar with its use. If yours is a bumper jack, consider a replacement. Hydraulic bottle jacks are safer and faster to use because they lift the wheel rather than the sprung weight of the car.

Install a locking gas cap. They not only keep thieves from stealing your gas, but nobody can put foreign material into your tank, thus causing your engine to die while they follow you from a shopping mall.

Don't go anywhere without fix-a-flat. It not only fixes slow leaks by re-sealing the tire-to-rim bead, but it saves time you may have to spend on the road changing a flat.

Look into a defensive driving school. They're scattered around the country and teach advanced driving technique. These schools can be tough on vehicles, so it's a good idea to rent one similar to your own for school. Of course, get full insurance.

If you want to do your best defensive driving, pump up your tires with a can of easy flat repair you get from most auto parts stores. Use four cans. You may be sliding sideways and you don't want to lose a hub cap or have a tire collapse because you don't have enough bead-to-rim tire pressure.

Do not leave your auto registration in your glove compartment or over your visor. That used to be the accepted practice; no more. Today's computers prove you own the car. Use a plastic baggie, and hide your registration. For example, you may want to bury it under the rubber mats in the trunk, or tape it up under the dash in a tough place to find. Why? Same reason you hide your garage door opener. Thieves in shopping malls search for garage door openers in your car, smash your window, take the opener and your registration. **Does your auto registration show your home address?** If that be the case, you may have unwittingly invited some burglars to your garage. They'll drive in, push-button the door behind them, and if need be, use your tools to break through a wall. You'll wonder how they burglarized your house and left so quickly.

Personalized license plates are a bad idea, especially for women. They're too easy to remember. Lot's of rapes occur to women of status because of the feeling of conquest involved. Important women with personalized plates may appear to be a bigger conquest. Don't attract attention to yourself or your car. Also, don't have any "BABY ON BOARD" signs in the windows, because those signs could invite a kidnapper. Any confrontational bumper stickers or signs might make someone mad---especially if you make a mistake in traffic.

Express yourself at the polls, not on the highway. Remember how religion and politics are to be avoided in polite conversation? To avoid controversy, keep the rear bumper or back window of your family van clean. You never know what is going to set off some already-troubled half-wit. Keep in mind that a percentage of the jerks you see on the road use physical violence to win conflicts with wives at home. Why should it be any different with you? Go out of your way not to offend anyone on the road.

FIREARMS IN THE VEHICLE

Keep at least one defensive firearm in your vehicle at all times. Do everything you can to avoid a violent confrontation but be prepared to defend yourself. Whatever defense weapon you choose to bring with you, take a supply of ammo. Don't just throw some shells in the car. Take Sunday go-to-meetin' super-stoppers so you load the weapon for war rather than birds or target shooting.

Don't expect to get special treatment as a good citizen if you get caught breaking a weapons law. Many prosecutors are into numbers. Whether they catch a gang member or a citizen violating gun laws doesn't matter; a conviction is a conviction. A gang member goes to prison to be with his friends—but your conviction sends you into a hostile atmosphere. Therefore, gang members don't care about gun laws, but good citizens have real reason to obey. Police departments are also into numbers; an arrest is an arrest. Because of this, **never** give permission to anyone to search your vehicle for any reason. The cop may be an expert at making you feel guilty, but don't give in. If you do, you probably waived your legal rights to the inclusion of any evidence the police find, no matter how it got there.

The question you think you have to answer is: Should you carry a weapon in the car with you? But that's the wrong question. The correct question is: Will I use this weapon if the need arises? To do that, you'll have to overcome your fear of jail, your good humanistic inhibitions, and a lack of proficiency with the firearm. Don't avoid thinking your way through the issue. Here's why: If you don't think you can use a weapon, don't carry it in the car. Without practice and firm mental resolve, a weapon can be a liability. Is it best to do what the perp demands? Yes--- unless you think he'll kill you. In that event, go for it. You'll need lots of practice and a great holster, but you could beat a perp who doesn't suspect you're armed.

In a personal interview with the LAPD, the Downtown Division Crime Prevention officer told us this: After the riot in South Central, people in L. A. were buying weapons in record numbers. But few practice enough to be quick and accurate with the weapons they buy. Moreover, people who buy the weapons "are too humanistic" to be able to kill another human easily. Therefore, there is a lag time by good people before they fire, but a hard-hearted, drugged-up criminal kills without hesitation. One more important reason for the critical lag time is this: Good citizens don't know the law but have an idea that anyone who uses a gun might be wrong. The enemy, on the other hand, knows about criminal punishment and he's not afraid. If he feels afraid, he often overcomes that fear with drugs. Thus you can believe, in any gun battle with a criminal, you'll come out second best unless you practice and develop a hardened mind set.

How does the LA. Police Dept. define practice? "Shoot a thousand rounds a year." Better than a mere thousand rounds punching holes through paper, pistol shooting instructor Stuart Meredith says, "Practice has to put pressure on the student. The idea is to force the secretion of adrenaline by approximating real excitement." I agree. When you practice, try to prepare yourself for the heart-pounding fear you'll face in a real encounter.

All this book (any book) can do is provide information. We encourage you to practice and develop speed and resolve. Even if you make some mistakes and the other side lives to concoct a great lie in court under oath, think about this:

Better to be judged by twelve (jurors)
than carried by six (pallbearers).

If you decide to carry a weapon, improve your driving habits. Don't do anything which might require an officer to search you or your vehicle. Of course, don't drink and drive. Never allow any passenger to open a container in your car. Keep documentation for the vehicle in proper order. Keep your concealed weapons carry permit current. When stopped by a police officer, it's a good idea to roll down your driver's side window and put both hands out into the light. Lay your wrists over the window ledge, which shows you have no evil intentions and puts the officer at ease. Never argue! They don't need the experience and the job doesn't pay any better because of flak they take from you. Always be polite and courteous when questioned. If you disagree with him or her, argue in court.

Now, after reading this, if you've decided to carry a weapon with you in your vehicle, let's think about what it should be. First, how's your size and strength? Many people buy bigger weapons for their car than they can handle comfortably. Bigger caliber weapons can tempt you because they are more powerful and you don't have to carry the weight personally. But people tend to put off practice when they own a big banger. Lack of practice increases your reaction time in a confrontation. Just buy what you know you can shoot without flinching at the noise and recoil; then, practice---a lot.

Handgun or shotgun? For vehicle travel, you need to operate your weapon with one hand so handguns are best. Reduced length shotguns with folding stocks are OK, but only if you ride as passenger.

Driving alone. Wrap the pistol in a flimsy cloth to disguise it. You can shoot right through any knit or sock. Once you've accessed the weapon, it will look like a sock or some kind of knitting in your hand. Hopefully, you won't have to shoot, and nobody will notice it. Another way to carry is under the seat in a (cigar?) box. Put a piece of cord to the box and attach the end of the cord to

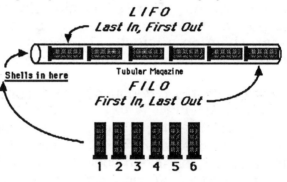

velcro near your feet. That way, a short pull on the cord puts the weapon where you can grab it easily, but it normally stays back, out of sight.

What about caliber? We like the .357 magnum revolver because its projectiles are capable of penetrating car bodies, which may be necessary to stop attackers in a vehicle. Automatics may bounce hot shell casings off your windshield. Also, a malfunction problem with an auto could easily require two hands to correct, which is difficult during evasive driving.

87

You can purchase a package of six specialty rounds. Tracers leave a bright trail behind the bullet path. Load tracers near the end of your firing string so you get advance notice to prepare for reloading---with either a new magazine or speed loader.

Pump and Semi-auto shotguns are LIFO loaders. LIFO means Last In, First Out. The last round you load will be the first to fire. The first round in will be last out.

Load accordingly. In a close range confrontation, you'll want shot first, maybe slugs later. In your house, you won't want to penetrate a wall with a load of heavy shot. Rifled slugs are heaviest and therefore penetrate well. Double ought (00-Buck) buck loads are commonly used by prison guards. They shoot nine .30 caliber balls, each lethal, and the spread of the shot is sure to score somewhere on a target. The best shotgun load for home defense is a high base shell with a load of two's or four's. For vehicles, however, you may need more distance and penetration. Go to double-ought buck or slugs.

LAPD warns: "Turn up your perception knob." But that's not all you do. You also have to stay ready. Don't get too tired, let your blood sugar drop. Finally, don't get into a position where you can't use your hands. Recently, Huber was guarding a young girl from a royal family as she shopped in a Washington, D.C. mall. She handed him some packages to carry. He refused, and explained, " I would like to be helpful, but I can't do my job if my hands are full."

When you come out of a shopping mall, your hands will probably be full, too. First, check the perimeter---the area around the store. Is anybody paying more attention to you than you deserve? If you sense trouble, trust your instincts; go back into the mall and ask a security guard to watch you until get into your car. If you go it alone, consider a shopping cart. They make folding ones you can carry into a store. That means only one hand is occupied with packages, and you can drop the handle easily to react to a situation. Do you suspect you're being followed while still on foot? If you have the time to get into your car and get away, do that. But if your stalker is close, opening your own car door is a bad idea. Act as if you can't find your car and make three consecutive right or left turns. If the same person is behind you, get ready for war. Walk towards others because there is safety in numbers. Duck behind a vehicle to get your weapon(s) ready. Failing that, start attracting attention. Work your way back into the mall where you can call for security. Never act scared. Don't ignore the threat. If you can't slip back into the mall or move near a crowd, it's frontal assault time. Turn around and confront the stalker. Tell him you have a gun, shoot well, and are about to blow him away.

Don't make deals. Criminals lie convincingly. Don't ever think you can do what this person tells you and thus save yourself. You can't be kind to them and expect kindness in return. If you're already in your car and you're told to move over, and let the perp into the driver's seat, **don't!** Step on the gas hard! Your chances of ducking a bullet while in a moving vehicle are excellent. Don't let anyone get in the car with you, but if it happens and he orders you to drive, just get nervous--and crash into another car, preferably in the presence of a cop. With this new set of circumstances, the perpetrator has some tough choices. He can shoot you in front of a crowd or get out and run.

Lock your car doors. Always! If your windows are tinted well and your doors are locked, nobody can get into your car or see you. Your car is actually a fairly secure fortress if you lock the doors. An added benefit: Locking your doors will help prevent you from being thrown from the vehicle in the event of an accident. It also keeps children from accidentally opening the car door while under way.

Buckle your seat belt. It helps you stay in control if you have to do a bit of defensive driving. If someone does open your door and tries to pull you from the vehicle, the seat belt will hold you in place while you step on the gas. Make sure all your passengers are belted in, too, so they don't fly into you during a defensive driving situation.

Don't leave loose packages lying about in the passenger compartment. Especially don't keep anything in the rear window well. Keep heavy items securely tied down or stored in the trunk. You don't want missiles whipping about your head if you're forced to take evasive action or crash your vehicle .

Keep your fuel level high. If you should happen to get into driving trouble with one of the growing number of morons on the interstate, you'll need extra gas. It'll be a comfort to have enough fuel to make the nearest police barracks or to keep driving long enough to get away.

Having a little extra fuel in the tank also allows you to drive on by if a chosen gas station is full of shady-looking characters. You'll be safer to stop at the first decent station you see after your tank gets about half empty. If you pay cash in advance, learn to put an even amount in your tank, or use the quick credit card so you need not wait for change.

No matter where you go or for how long, tell somebody; leave a note. Standard procedure in many households is to post a small blackboard near the inside of the front door where spouses and kids send messages and love notes. Then, if you don't return on time, your loved ones can notify police.

If your car breaks down, stay with the vehicle. Think of it as a turtle shell. If someone offers to give you a ride to a service station, decline. Hang a towel or scarf from your side mirror and wait for a state trooper or other emergency service vehicle. Don't leave your vehicle, don't get in anyone else's vehicle.

When you drive, pay close attention to what's happening on all four sides of your vehicle. Scan both side mirrors and your rear view every few minutes. Don't follow the cars in front of you too closely. If you do, you'll pay too much attention to traffic ahead of you and break the good habit of scanning your rear views.

Avoid restrooms in rest areas, many of which are now routinely patrolled by thieves and perverts. Homeless people often live there. If you absolutely need a restroom, restaurants and truck stops are safer than public facilities.

Men: Avoid urinals. You're extremely vulnerable to attack when standing with your back to the world in that circumstance. Use the toilet compartments and lock the door behind you. If no door, stand to the side. Thieves look first for a pair of pants dropped around shoes. Then they quietly climb on the seat in the next stall to grab the coat or bag you left hanging on the hook.

Women: Don't put your purse on the floor, on a hook or on the sink next to you. Keep it securely on your person. Females also prey upon rest stop travelers. It's best to carry a purse with a shoulder strap and set it on your lap.

Above all, **DON'T PICK UP HITCHHIKERS!** Thousands of bright people make this mistake each year; some pay with their lives. In most states it's not only against the law to hitchhike, it's against the law to pick them up. Don't be fooled by the gas can trick, either. The real criminals know how to make themselves look most pathetic. The better they fool you, the more macho they feel.

Stranded motorists are likewise a risk to you. Don't stop on the highway to give help. Even someone lying on the road could be setting a trap for you. Use your cellular phone or CB and call for help. In some of the latest capers, the germs got a girlfriend with a baby to stand by a "stranded" car with the hood up while they waited in the bushes a few yards away. It turned out to be an armed robbery for a good Samaritan on the highway.

All of us think of our vehicles as private space. That's no longer true. Drivers are easy prey for criminals. But turn up your perception knob, make a few additions to your vehicle, and stay locked behind tinted glass. You'll avoid most highway robbers and street thugs.

CONVICT---LOSS OF RIGHT TO SUE

Conviction for a crime automatically has to wipe out the criminal's standing to litigate. As it stands, our system is unfair. Convicts break in, beat up, rob, and rape their victims. If they get hurt in the process, they sue their victims from prison. They get a free law library along with plenty of time to sue anyone for anything. Meanwhile, the lawsuit robs the victim's peace of mind, costs attorneys fees to defend and drains the victims' ability to earn a livelihood. The standing to sue anyone must be lost upon a criminal's conviction.

Chapter 7

HOW TO REDUCE RISKS WHILE TRAVELING

On public transportation, the sophistication of the crime goes up with the cost of travel. Bus and train stations get bums and weirdoes; first-class air fare on a Concorde might put you in the path of a con artist. Buses carry some animals you can't believe. One police search of an interstate bus recently yielded several weapons and enough drugs to fill a briefcase. On the other hand, you can be pretty sure you won't encounter a weapon on an airplane. As a general rule, cheap travel puts <u>you</u> at risk; expensive travel puts <u>your property</u> at risk.

Another factor is the crowds. With a lot of people around, crimes against persons don't occur as often. But you have to watch out for your property. If they can grab your purse or your bag, they'll disappear into the crowd and be difficult to chase.

Overall, the same defense principles you apply elsewhere apply when traveling. Avoiding crime in transit is much the same as avoiding crime anywhere—-with a few new variations on the theme.

Don't drive away from your home city with your dealer's license plate frame on your car. Doing that will make your car a target for burglary. In San Diego, at Sea World, for example, Oakland dealer plates tell a car burglar you're a tourist---not likely to drive hundreds of miles to testify about your stolen golf clubs or camera in court.

In most tourist areas, criminals can steal property without much fear of prosecution. Hawaiian car rental agencies will tell you to leave your car empty with the trunk open and carry everything on your person. Why? Because thieves will break open the trunk and damage the car beyond the value of the goods they steal. Car burglary in Hawaii is profitable. Even if the criminal gets caught, the victim doesn't want to fly back from the mainland to testify after his vacation. But the minute the germs start messing with the tourists, themselves, all hell breaks loose. On Oahu, two armed robbers on a backpackers' trail were apprehended and sentenced to 24 years.

So—tourists should be most concerned about theft. Who steals? All kinds of people, although low class, rough looking transients will be prime suspects. But don't be fooled by appearances. The typical nice, old, lady can be an accomplished thief. Thieves frequently have a drug motivated need for more money than a highly paid executive can make. Women with the same drug needs get cash in other ways, but they can also be thieves when employed as maids, clerks in hotels, etc. If you travel cheaply, then you can expect the employees of the firms you'll be dealing with to be in a lower economic bracket. Guard your goods; dress down to the level of your traveling companions; don't flash any money or jewelry. In a motel, use the safe or vault. Failing, that, get creative in the art of hiding valuables.

Once you understand that danger levels change as your modes of transportation change, you can consider some of the different ways to travel. Then, make your defense plans against crime accordingly. No matter how you travel though, you'll be spending some time on foot, whether it's walking for a purpose, or exercising.

ON FOOT
If you walk much and your neighborhood is rough, don't carry valuables; carry defensive weapons. Purses

attract thieves like sticky paper attracts flies. Walk against traffic. In Los Angeles during August, 1992, one of the violent fatalities was a 94 year old grandmother with $8 in her purse. Purse snatchers in a car dragged her 100 feet to her death.

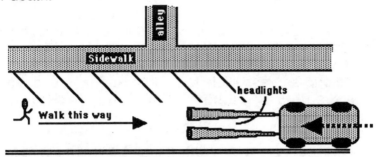

WALKING IN PAIRS
AREAS OF RESPONSIBILITY

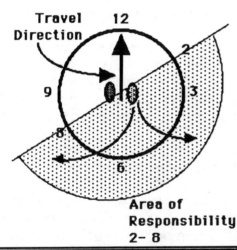

Day or night, don't walk on the right side of the road. Even if up on a sidewalk, walk on the left---**against** traffic. You're safer to walk in the middle of the sidewalk than on either edge, too, because most of the crud hiding in alleys can get you easily if you brush by. Those who do attack can't corner you as easily as they can on the inner edge of the sidewalk. Use the clock system to identify danger if in pairs. In addition to the above, stay on main streets. At night, don't travel where it's dark.

When bodyguards work a detail, each has an area of responsibility. You should, too. One of you watches the right and rear, from 2 - 8 on your defense clock. The other scans the front, <u>from 7 - 3</u>. Be professional; overlap.

95

Dress for combat more than looks. You can fight freely and run fast in tennis shoes and loose-fitting pants. Tight skirts and high heels leave you at a disadvantage.

As much as possible, don't walk or ride around alone. Many street criminals work in pairs. They have more nerve that way, and they actually fight nastier because each tries to impress the other. Besides that, they're afraid of losing. Seldom will they attack a superior number. So two or three in your group are less likely to be attacked than one alone. "There's safety in numbers," also applies to crime prevention.

Another great advantage to travelling in pairs: Broader range of weaponry. One carries short range weapons, the other carries long range. One carries gas, the other carries firepower. Warn each other about danger.

When you notice a rowdy group a block away and moving towards you on your side of the street, walk across the street or into an occupied building without attracting attention to yourself. When you can't avoid such a group, approach them with your head up and seek eye contact with one member of the group. Remain calm. Do not display fear but at the same time don't create a challenge that might require a response from them. "Dissin" is street talk for disrespect, and you would be surprised at how little it takes to incite a gang attack, especially when you're alone.

In a crowded area, prevent pickpockets from ripping you off by sewing Velcro on your pockets. When a pickpocket lifts the flap, the ripping noise tells you what happened, and tells him you know.

In transit, from bus to airport, van to bus station, etc. don't allow anyone not in porter's uniform to handle your baggage. If a stranger does handle your bags, chances are he'll run with them or extort a tremendous fee for carrying.

WHILE SLEEPING IN A HOTEL

Choose a ground floor room so you eliminate the need for using elevators or stairwells at night. On upper floors, ask for a room away from elevators. This makes the room less attractive to thieves because the escape route is longer. Don't take calls from hotel maintenance unless you get a clearance from security. Some hotel victims have let uniformed maintenance people into their room---only to find out they were imposters who first called, then beat and robbed them.

Improve security by staying in the room while it's being serviced by cleaning staff. Keep expensive cameras, watches, and jewelry out of sight whenever hotel staff are in the room. Place room service dishes outside your room and thus eliminate one more reason for staff to enter. With duct tape and plastic baggies, stick valuables to the undersides of desks, drawers or other furniture. Otherwise, use the hotel's safe.

Inform the hotel operator **not** to ring your room, but to take messages only. This makes it hard for anyone to find out whether you're there or not. Keep the security latch or chain on at all times. Leave the "Do Not Disturb" sign on the outside of the door. Close curtains on the entrance wall, especially when absent. Leave a TV or radio talk show station on when you leave. Do all of the above, and your motel stay should be reasonably safe.

SLEEPING ON THE GO

If you sleep while traveling on a bus, ferry, etc., sneak a secure line (parachute cord) to your pack or briefcase where nobody can see it; then tie that line off where a slight tug on it will wake you but a hard yank won't throw you off balance. Use a coin locker if you'll be spending several hours in an airport or train station. But then park your carcass where you can keep an eye on your locker. Lots of coin lockers are ripped off by people who rent the locker, then make a copy of the key.

When sleeping on planes and trains, keep tickets and other valuables in your inside coat pocket. Place your carry-on bag under the seat in front of you and put your feet on the bag while you sleep. With shoes off, you'll be much more sensitive to any movement.

AIRPORTS, BUS AND TRAIN STATIONS
Women, keep your checks and tickets in a handbag or briefcase. Shoulder bags with heavy straps make a lot of sense for the female traveler. They make it difficult for a thief to grab your bag and run. With the bag over your shoulder, then covered with a coat, they can't see your purse, much less snatch it.

Form an alliance if you're alone. Just make sure the person you pick is reliable. Choose women over men, clean over dirty, well-dressed over shabby. Recently, I flew from Hawaii to LA. then took a van downtown to catch a Greyhound bus into the desert. I was pass-out tired, and my bus wouldn't leave for two and a half hours. I saw two teenage girls with bags huddled in the corner, more scared than I. In a quick interview, I learned they were from England. They'd come here to be nannies at a children's camp, saved their money, and were touring through the USA. I needed rest so I said, "Let's make a deal. I'll plop down here and sleep; you watch my bags and warn me if a problem develops. Tell anybody who comes around that I just got out of the mental hospital in Camarillo and they should be extra quiet. If they bother either of us, I'll take them apart." The girls were wide-eyed and more than happy to stand watch. I rigged a line from my backpack to my belt loop and covered it. My tote bag was my pillow. We moved to a strategic corner, and I dreamed away.

The same general plan works in youth hostels, air terminals, on ferries etc. If more than one party has access

98

to your quarters, and you're alone, do a little interview work and find someone you can team up with and trust. Try to make sure that one stays awake while the other sleeps.

ON A BIKE

I took a bike ride around San Diego recently. I was a cop there and I know the city pretty well. By talking to a lot of new homeless people who moved to Balboa park, I learned things are tough. Drugs abound. Car burglary is common. Nights are dangerous.

If you pedal to a San Diego store in daylight and leave your bike without locking it, kiss it good-bye. You can tell how many are stolen by the street price of a 10-speed. Under $15. All a thief has to do is jump on and go.

Bike riders not only need to watch their wheels; they need to take care of themselves. In a pinch without any other weapon, your bike pump used as a pool-cue penetrator or a club will give you *some* help, at least.

If you ride alone, you can take your mountain bike into the wilderness and be fairly safe from crime. You can disappear into the woods, and nobody knows you're there unless you make a lot of noise or burn a smoky fire. You can also ride with a group and enjoy safety in numbers. But if you ride alone and travel down streets in a bad part of town or on a secluded bike path in a city park, watch out. Ambush is a distinct possibility when you ride past bushes and trees. One sideways shove and you're down. Anything more and you may not get up.

In cities and countries with little crime (notably Canada), you can ride on the right side of the road. Drivers don't want an accident, and most will steer clear. Where the crime problem is real, though, ride the way you walk—against traffic. You can't afford to get hit from behind. On a country road, you can always ditch. In a city, go up on the sidewalk or pull in between parked cars and stop.

When you ride against traffic, watch out at driveways and corners! Drivers will be looking for traffic from the opposite direction only. Wear a helmet, too. In a fight, you can duck your chin and an incoming blow bouncing off a bike helmet won't do damage to anything but your assailant's fist.

TAKING CABS

Never get in a cab unless you first ask how much the fare is. In the Philippines, the answer for fare to Clark Air Force Base was, "Oh, it's a short trip, you can pay me what you want." Then, after we arrived, fifteen Filipinos surrounded my cab while the driver tried to extort big bucks from me. We settled, of course, but I lost money.

When taking a cab by yourself in a foreign country, sit directly behind the driver. Order him to lock all the doors. In the Philippines and Mexico, drivers often go to a place where they meet a gang of twenty. Routinely, when I worked as a cop on the Tijuana border, we would see badly beaten sailors dumped back at the border in skivvies only. In Thailand, I traveled with a Green Beret buddy who always sat behind the driver. One day a cab driver made a wrong turn into a dark and cruddy section of town, but a very sharp pen knife caused the driver to stop, back it up, and drive in a new direction. As the cab pulled out on a main street again, the knife disappeared. Later, my buddy had the driver stop in front of a cop; we got out and paid for the ride in plain sight. It was a polite encounter.

ON THE BUS

This is now a dangerous way to travel in the U.S. I always wonder about the drivers---they look so respectable. But they settled the last strike by using snipers to pepper the buses. Bus travel is cheap, which may be why the terminals are human junk yards. Some of the travelers scare me. On a bus, feel free to change your seat as the situation demands. You don't have to stay in one place. If you ride in the back, nobody sits behind you. Moving to the front may provide safety in numbers.

Bus and train terminals see lots of scams. Most have to do with ticket exchanges. Don't buy tickets from anyone but the airlines or rail ticket office. One of the most prevalent scams works like this: A presentable-looking individual will approach you and explain that his or her wallet or purse has been stolen along with their tickets. They have a Rolex or Nikon or something worth a great deal more than the cost of the ticket they need. If you're willing to buy them a ticket, they will give you the "item" for security. When they get home they will send you the money for the ticket plus $100 and you can return their property. Sure. . Either the property is stolen or it's a fake.

Keep your distance from strangers. Don't let them lead you into a conversation. Get tactically situated if you have to wait. Corners are good, as are seats against a wall. If you're waiting in a long line and someone scary gets behind you, address the situation. Say, "Are you waiting to buy a ticket?" If the answer is yes, say, "Go ahead of me, please. My bus won't be leaving for a long time." You need to stand <u>behind</u> suspicious persons, <u>not in front</u>.

With luggage in the overhead rack, you'd best stay awake. If you're really tired, move your bags to a window seat, then sleep leaning up against them from an aisle seat.

In a foreign country, buses and trains are somewhat safer. Even so, I make an alliance with somebody before I sleep. I once took my 10-year old boy on a train trip deep in Mexico through the Tarajumara Indian country. I speak fluent Spanish and made friends with a *Cabo* (corporal) in the *federales*. I taught him a few things about his German assault rifle. We slept in shifts and I never lost a dime.

<u>NOTES ON FOREIGN TRAVEL</u>
Why not go somewhere nice—-where you don't have

to worry about crime? What parts of the world are most crime-free? As it happens, English is spoken there. New Zealand is a country with a tradition of peace, friendliness and propriety. In Australia, I stayed in a rough neighborhood and found it free of crime. Parts of Canada are also nice— notably Vancouver Island, B.C., which is full of people who are lovely to the core. On the other hand, some Canadian cities are now a little rough. Hawaii is not crime free. Parts of Oahu are downright dangerous. If you want to experience the feeling of a lone black person at a white country club in the South, try to surf with Hawaiian locals on their beach. You're a haole; they've bruised many badly.

Europe has its fair share of crime. Besides, you have to hassle with the petty crooks who take advantage of the language barrier. In Italy, once, a 16 year old sweetheart of a girl shortchanged me and I caught her at it. *"Mire,"* I said, as I held the coin up, *"Cinque, cinque."* (Look, five, five!) Oh—-she was so embarrassed. She took back my coin and gave me some others, which I dumped in my pocket. "Got to get up real early to fool me," I thought. Later, after I'd left the cafeteria, I recounted the money; she'd short changed me worse the second time.

Mexico can be a little tough, especially in the border towns. Labor is cheap, and so is life in some parts. On the other hand, country folk there are genuine. The general rule to apply when you travel in a foreign country is to look around. Your first clue: See if the bicycles are locked. In Fussa, just South of Tokyo, Japan, whole racks of bikes outside a department store had no locks on them. The crime rate there was low. In Guatamala recently I went into a bank and saw a guard there with a machine gun. I spoke to him and asked why he was armed that heavily. *"Hay muchos ladrones,* (There are many thieves.) he said. He wore a bullet proof vest, too. Likewise, when you see burglar bars on windows or barbed wire on the top of fences, the neighborhood contains germs. Be on guard.

In any foreign country, each family member needs to have close-up, clear photos of all others in a file folder in case one gets lost or kidnapped. Make half tones so you can make hundreds of copies on any copier to spread the word around fast in an emergency.

If you want to see some real crime, visit Washington D.C. or many major U.S. cities. You can sit on a porch near the White House on any given night and enjoy the gunfire. Also, St. Croix, U.S. Virgin Islands is rough. After Hurricane Hugo, even the police and National Guard were looting. Today, the same criminal mentality is all over, and visiting tourists cannot carry guns, so crime is profitable.

IN THE AIR

Air travel usually offers fewer problems than cheaper forms of transportation. Not only do you mix 'n mingle with a higher class of passenger, but inspections make theft less easy. Carry on as much baggage as you can. Baggage handlers are poorly paid employees who sometimes supplement their income. For check in, I use inexpensive luggage in which I keep a candle. Drop a little hot candle wax to make a seal on your baggage locks and you'll be able to tell if the bag was opened since you saw it last. Another way, either pull a hair from your head or a match out of a matchbook. Hang one of these half in and out of the case so they barely protrude when closed. If it's gone when you land, your luggage was opened.

Overstuffed luggage is frequently dropped by handlers because they know it will pop open so they can pilfer a few items. Put an ID tag (no home address) inside your luggage. People who steal luggage around airports often cut outside ID tags off. You can identify your bags more easily with your ID hidden inside.

In the terminal, use the dining and rest room facilities located inside the security check points. Crime is less prevalent there. Board the plane early while the overhead storage is empty. Store your carry-ons directly over <u>your</u> seat; otherwise they may be gone when you land. Be careful about what you put in the overhead storage compartments. Someone could grab your stuff while pretending to get something out of their own gear. Put a spare toothbrush and paste, a razor, and one clean change of clothes in your carry-on baggage in case your checked-in bags get sent by mistake to Egypt. It happens all the time.

ON THE BEACHES

TWO MATCHING TOWELS SEWN

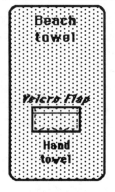

Buy a beach towel and a hand towel made of the same material. Then, sew the two together so the smaller towel makes a color blend-in pocket with Velcro flap on the big one. Carry your beach goodies in there. With the pocket on the sandy side, nobody will see it. Even if you have to go for your gun because you suspect trouble, it will look as if you're wiping your hands. If the trouble really develops, you don't have to display the weapon. Just shoot a hole right through the terry cloth.

On the beach carry your car keys, money, ID, and a loaded stainless steel handgun in a plastic ziplock baggie. Be careful though if you leave your weapon sealed in plastic for a long time, salt air moisture will search out and rust any unprotected part. Even though you swim a lot, you won't lose anything. Why? Look around, and when nobody is watching, bury it all a few inches below the surface beneath your towel. Then go into the water, and return to the towel. After you dry off, dig the baggie out. As soon as you get a chance, spray your weapon well with an oil-based coating.

GENERAL RULES

When traveling, never carry more cash than necessary. Of course, make sure to have enough cash to satisfy a mugger. You can't afford to make one mad at you. Carry traveler's checks and use credit cards you can replace. Your responsibility for charges on the cards ends as soon as you report them stolen. You would think that's good news, but it's the opposite.

During research for this book, I flew to New Orleans with a sheriff who told me victims in the French Quarter were being robbed, then shot. The police couldn't figure out why. We learned: <u>Some fences will pay a higher price for a stolen credit card when they learn the victim died, because dead victims can't cancel credit cards.</u>

Fix this in advance. Don't keep your credit cards in your wallet or purse. Slice a hole in your jacket pocket and slip them into the lining, or, shove them down into a sock. Toss all your important documents---licenses, ID's and credit cards, list of traveler's checks serial numbers, plus the serial numbers of any computers, cameras, guns etc---on a copier and push the button. Copy both sides. If you don't report in on time, have your cards canceled and the local police informed of the card and I.D. numbers. That should help apprehend any robber. It *might* also save your life when you explain that canceling is automatic and try to bargain.

Never discuss your plans with hotel staff. Many hotel employees drink in local bars and may be an information peddler. Also, don't draw attention to yourself by either over tipping or not tipping at all. If you don't tip enough, you become a subject of sore discussion between the angry maid you stiffed and someone at the bar who's listening to how rich and stingy you are. Tip too much, and they talk about you, the rich, big spender. Either way, you may become a target.

A little research on the local laws about weapons and defense is doubly important when you're visiting a foreign country. Undocumented firearms can mean real trouble.

Learn to depend on other defense measures when you can't carry a handgun. You can almost always carry a knife. Check it in at airports and you retrieve it when you land. Make sure yours opens with one hand. (See **Everybody's Knife Bible.**) You can also make a Bo or a short club with the clothes rack bar out of your hotel room when you go jogging. With a saw blade or knife, you can make a decent weapon out of any broom. Roll the handle and tap on the back of a knife blade to knock it progressively into the wood and get a clean cut.

Be aware of everything going on around you all the time. Train yourself to look for something out of place or someone out of line. Long coats worn in hot summer times can mean weapons concealed underneath. Look at the pictures of criminals on TV and newspapers. Some ladies make their statements of elegance; street criminals' dress makes a statement of a common astrological sign, *feces.* When you're out on the street, the germs' dress code may be all the warning you get. Remember, if it feels bad, it probably is.

Think about what you can do if a violent situation develops. Don't let your loved ones walk into a trap. Planticipate. You're a good bodyguard when you keep out of trouble. Former cops and Karate pros don't always make good bodyguards. Even though so many police cars feature the "Protect and Serve" motto, that's not what cops do. "Protect" is something you do for someone before trouble starts, or at least during. If all you do is take a report afterwards and begin to search for the perpetrators, you're protecting nobody. Karate people focus on what to do during trouble. To work their magic, they have to wait for an attack. That's not bodyguarding. Want to be your own bodyguard? Think ahead---and avoid problems.

Because of so much crime in society now, rules of courtesy have changed. Be conscious of your loved ones' safety. Men, ask your wives to drive. You be her passenger and bodyguard; load as a LIFO loader---First In, Last Out. She gets in, starts the car, and you, (Last In) check for trouble before you jump in and go. When she stops, hop out right away and look around. Think, "security."

AT CROWDED PUBLIC EVENTS
Be careful in a crowd. Make it a point to carry only tickets, driver's license, and a small amount of cash whenever you go to ball games or races (auto or horse). Carry these in your front pants pocket. Since fanny packs have become popular, some street germs use a sharp knife to cut the strap and run. A small 4" web belt velcro-attached around the fanny pack strap and the belt on your slacks prevents immediate removal, and gives you enough time to extract your weapon.

Ladies, don't wear jewelry to ball games or races. Blend in with the crowd. Don't wear anything or do anything which might draw the attention of thieves. Remember, employees at public events often come from a labor pool that is part time. Some sell information. Also, criminals act on victims and property targets of opportunity. If you don't present that opportunity, you may save yourself a lot of pain.

***

As crime becomes more prevalent, travel is more risky. Still, you may have to go somewhere to do something you can't do through the mail or over the phone. Apply the precautions and tricks in this chapter, and your chances of having a safe and enjoyable trip will be much improved.

107

CRIMINALS' FUTURES AS A BALANCE FOR SOCIETY

To make society in the U.S. better balanced, criminal courts have to change. In addition to looking at the deed, itself, they also must take a close look at the victim and perpetrator. Thus, if the "victim" appeared only to be trespassing but had a record of arrests and convictions, and the "perpetrator" appeared to be an aggressor who shot while in his or her own home, the prior-to-crime status quo of each citizen would add balancing weight to the event and its trial.

Furthermore, couldn't a judge or jury find from personal histories a certain future probability of status of each person in society? When one has been an honest 35 year old citizen all of her life, the probability of her continuing to contribute for the next 35 years is strong. On the other hand, a welfare bum with six convictions and 25 arrests during the first one third of his lifetime will probably double his trouble during his last two thirds of life.

Looking at only evidence submitted on the bare facts of a case without considering the parties' histories and probable future crimes commission tips courtroom decisions in a wrong direction.

WHEN A MOTHER BREEDS CRIMINALS

Let the legislatures define financial AID TO DEPENDENT MOTHERS: It's a grant from the state given to a deserving mother for producing a good, productive member for our society. If the child is not loved, trained and nurtured so that he or she becomes good and productive, should the mother still collect the money? Moreover, what if that child becomes a beast and preys upon us, and proves between the ages of 11 to 18 that his ~~mother~~ person who gave birth did worse than no job. Shouldn't all or part of the grant be taken away from her?

The way it appears to be in Brooklyn, New York, for many mothers now, it's an annuity for prostitution. The by-products of mothers' sex-for-state-payment run wild and create havoc with society. By 1999, over 80% of one minority's children will be illegitimate. An L.A. deputy sheriff who worked the gang detail for years told me the motto for mothers who give birth to illegitimate children:

"Every kid is a paycheck."

When I did the original research on rape for *Everybody's Knife Bible*, I talked with Hawaiian prosecutors on the issue of dealing the crime down to a lesser offense in exchange for a plea of guilty. Prosecutors often agree to deal on rape charges because defense attorneys almost always threaten them with a lengthy trial. Understaffed prosecutors' offices continuously contend with felons' petitions for dismissal because of infringement on their right to a speedy trial. So a long trial in a rape case puts other cases in jeopardy. Defense attorneys know this and use the threat-of-long-trail tactic a lot. *Don*

Chapter 8
How to...
DEFEND AGAINST RAPE AND ASSAULT

THREAT OF RAPE---THE ENEMY'S MIND SET.

The attitude many men adopt from looking at women purely out of lust and therefore without regard for her, the person, is demeaning. If a man admires only a part of her, the rest becomes insignificant; therefore, he feels more significant. When attitudes like this are prevalent in a society, women are in trouble.

A rapist is often acting out a response to dysfunction, which he expresses in <u>power, control, anger, or sadism</u>. He wants revenge—-for the way he's been treated, the rejections he's suffered, and the scorn heaped upon him. Revenge means: He feels down; he sees rape as a way to get back up. <u>Your job</u>: Create a psychological atmosphere which will turn him off, sexually. Be a domineering, full-of-hate, screamer.

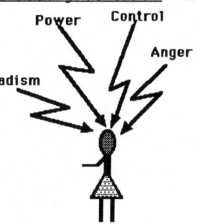

The same techniques used to defend against other types of attack often work well to defend you against sexual assault. More than with other crimes, however, the three time elements are vital. Against rape, there are things to do **before, during and after**. What you do during each time period affects what happens during the time period following. Before is important. Since this crime is so heinous, you need to take extra precautions.

RAPE BY ACQUAINTANCE

Since so many rapes are committed by perps who know their victims, let's take a look at some new ways to identify a problem male. Rape committed by someone you know seldom occurs with no warning. Rapists act in patterns you can identify, which we list below like storm warnings. As the storm of rape gets closer and the danger becomes more real, this goes on:

His eyes devour you. If you feel undressed by a man's eyes or frightened by the way he looks at you, take heed. Any leering in his visual contact should put you on notice. Be cautious with a man who won't look you directly in the eye and who stares at your body as if it were a target.

His mouth is out of control. Look for a demeaning comment, especially with reference to your body parts. Double *entendre* is his specialty. If you took it wrong; it's your fault. Maybe it will be a series of off-color remarks about sex, or even bathroom talk. Anything he puts out which might be considered by some to be complimentary will make you feel more debased than flattered. Direct address words such as "broad, hot chick, sex kitten, squeeze, etc., tip you off about attitude.

His hands roam. At first, it may only be a hand on your arm, but it makes you feel uncomfortable. If his touch feels terrible, you're in danger. Contact of a sexual nature feels decently OK if it's coupled with a transfer of caring and emotion. Sexual contact and foreplay devoid of that emotion will feel wrong and degrading---sort of icky. If it feels that way to you, it probably is; get out!

Fail to take note of <u>eyes, mouth, or hands</u> and serious trouble could be on your horizon. Don't ignore the signs. At work, it may be sexual harassment. If at work, document the problem (include date, time, details) in writing and send a sealed, hand postmarked copy to yourself and supervisors. From a date, it's a fishing expedition to find out whether or not you'll tolerate indecent conduct. Quit dating anyone you suspect.

If the trouble is in your home, seek help from a man of God---priest, minister or rabbi. You can also call a rape crisis center and consult a counselor. Home rapists are the worst, and they're never satisfied with just one contact; often it goes on for years. What's worse is this: He, with his older experience and more elderly position in your family, will make you feel as if it's your fault.

How does loveless sexual conduct come about? Playboys can't afford emotional involvement. To love one woman and have sex with another often creates guilt. To escape guilt, they simply avoid emotional involvement---they stay aloof. So far, so good, they think. But to avoid involvement, they also have to block out incoming emotion. Therefore, many playboys live a life without feeling loved, which produces a low self image. Not feeling worthy of love, and feeling a low self image, a man searches for a self-image boost. As the need for the boost increases and as the self image lowers, women become more unapproachable. Pornography appears to gratify but actually increases need and lowers image even further. Likewise, prostitute contact does the same.

With need up and image down, he doesn't relate well. You get rapport with him sometimes, but at other times, you lose it—severely. Sometimes he's nervous around you and you don't know why. Your sixth sense about this guy gives you a creepy feeling. Even though he appears to be normal, something is weird and you can't put your finger on it.

Three kinds of people are: 1. those who make things happen, 2. those to whom things happen, and 3. those who don't know what's happening. Look for signs of a manipulator. If he makes things happen, you may be the person to whom things happen. Such a person would put you on the defensive in a conversation, and would do a lot of things for no other reason than to impress you.

It's hard to tell how a man may act with you in a clinch if you haven't spent time with him. Just be careful. A man with a gentle and sensitive spirit shouldn't mind meeting you at a public place for a first date. You can take separate cars. Double dates are also a great idea. Date rape frequently occurs in the victim's apartment. Admit nobody until you know them.

Before you relax and let your guard down with a date, it's a good idea to meet and spend time with his family and friends. When a man has strong ties to a family with good values, he would probably be devastated by embarrassment if he were charged with rape. Along the same lines of thought, **beware** of a man other men don't like. Just as women know and understand each other, so do men. They relax and expose their inner thoughts more while talking man-to-man.

HOW TO DEFEND AGAINST RAPE AND ASSAULT FROM A STRANGER

If one fourth of American women are raped sometime during their lives and many go unreported, I guarantee, a lot of rapists roam freely among us. Being a woman today must be like being an enemy soldier in a guerrilla war zone. You can't tell who the enemy is and you have no idea where the next battle will take place. They can attack as they please (24 hours a day); all you can do is wait to defend. If I were one in a gathering of women, I would think, "which 'one-out-of-four' of us will be the next?"

WHAT ARE YOUR CHANCES?

Your chances of being the victim of <u>attempted</u> rape are one out of four during your lifetime. Those are the most reliable statistics we have, but nobody knows for sure. Key on the word, "<u>attempted</u>."

As any Green Beret will tell you, the best way to stay alive in a war zone is to ask yourself frequently, "What will I do if . . ?" To figure that, you have to find out what the "if's" might be. How do rapists operate? What might they do?

<u>Don't escape a rape, keep out of possible rape situations</u>. Avoid suspect people and dangerous places. Pay close attention to your surroundings, especially to men.

A good part of avoiding the crime of rape is in developing an <u>invincible</u> <u>mindset</u>. You **are not** going to be a victim!

If you have to get physically violent in order to save yourself, you made a mistake—-something an aware bodyguard wouldn't do. If you had to pull your gun or use a baseball bat, you let your guard down.

You can beat the rapists! To do that, repeat and reinforce the dysfunction which caused him to want power and control in the first place. If we can teach you what turns a rapist on, couldn't you learn how to flip that switch and turn him off? And---when you flip that switch off, could you do it forcefully? Let's see how the desire-to-rape develops.

I believe, that when you treat him coldly and command and dominate him, you impede the stranger-rapist's arousal. *Don*

Almost always, **human desires arise because of deprivation.** The desire to eat is enormous when deprived of food, and desire for warmth is intense when cold. What deprivations cause the desire to rape? Discover these and you have the key to safety: Instead of creating an atmosphere that will turn him on; turn him off.

If you appear to be weak, shy or fearful, you allow him to become excited. That's why so many rape defense classes teach you posture---head up, shoulders back and purposeful ways of walking. Women who take charge have a much better chance of staying out of rape's way if, on first contact, they dominate, use a loud, strong voice, and talk down at the potential perpetrator. If you're angry at the way women are treated in this society, a possible rape situation is a great time to let that anger come to the surface!

If you become psychologically powerful and gain control of the situation, you have a good chance of winning because encountering a superior power turns him off. Get your psychological power up and running first and be stronger during. This is a real contest of wills. A strong female authority figure somewhere in his personal history is often what caused his dysfunction. If you can turn him back into a frightened little boy, even for a moment, you can win. So, never give up. It's never over; you can win. One good, strong blow, coupled with self assurance and adrenal power, can push the situation to the right side of the circle, where you have a good chance of winning---or at least escaping while he tries to regain control.

CONTEST OF WILLS IN A RAPE SITUATION

He pushes → ← **She pushes**

She who pushes first and most strongly wins

THE PSYCHO-SEXUAL SITUATION
A CONTEST OF WILLS

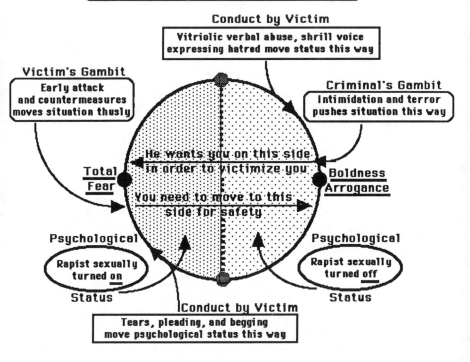

Conduct by Victim
Vitriolic verbal abuse, shrill voice expressing hatred move status this way

Victim's Gambit
Early attack and countermeasures moves situation thusly

Criminal's Gambit
Intimidation and terror pushes situation this way

He wants you on this side in order to victimize you

You need to move to this side for safety

Total Fear

Boldness Arrogance

Psychological
Rapist sexually turned on

Psychological
Rapist sexually turned off

Status

Status

Conduct by Victim
Tears, pleading, and begging move psychological status this way

PSYCHO-SEXUAL SITUATION

On the left half you see a psycho-sexual atmosphere which turns the rapist on. On the right, the psycho-sexual atmosphere turns him off. To escape rape, your job is to move the situation to the right. Sometimes you can't; but **you must try!**

It's like war---either kill or be killed. In rape, it's either you create more dysfunction for him, or he compensates for dysfunction by raping. If possible, follow the DefCon rules and be first. If not first, then be more resolute, stronger, and absolutely defiant If you can be both first and stronger, chances of succeeding increase a lot.

115

ACTIVE OR PASSIVE?

Consider passive defense, which might work for you, but you have to stay calm. Dropping into emotional fits or crying will arouse your attacker. Small talk might keep him off balance, but don't allow yourself to be moved or manipulated into a dark corner while you apply any stalling tactic. You can try a verbal counter measure, such as, "Here, take this money and go get a pro; I have AIDS."

Many rapists tell their victims: "Don't make any noise or I'll hurt you." Never comply; it's a sexual turn on he wants you to supply. Make all the noise you can. Screaming helps also because it's a natural way to get your own adrenaline flowing. Don't scream for help (causes arousal) scream at him! Be graphic as you describe the ways you are going to hurt him if he doesn't leave you alone. Doing that disconcerts the attacker, makes you stronger, and helps you overcome fear-induced paralysis. It wipes out a man turned on by power. Instead of being weak, submissive, and cooperative, you become a menace; that's a turn-off. Also, think about this. If you're not alone in a remote area, there is a chance that if you make a lot of noise and scream for help, someone will hear you and respond or at least call the police. Get all the attention you can.

Against rape by a stranger, take some extra precautions. Don't escape a rape, keep out of possible rape situations. Avoid suspect people and dangerous places. Rape occurs:

In the home. Attacker hides in home or garage and surprises you. Some break into the home at night. The majority of rapes occur here because a bold invasion of your most private space heightens a rapist's excitement, especially when it terrifies the victim.

In a car. Sometimes it happens by surprise in a

parking lot or dimly lit street. Abduction to a secluded area is also possible. Above all, don't let that happen.   If he threatens to shoot you, let him do it where other people are present and you can get immediate help and treatment.

> A large percentage of pistol gunshot wounds are **not** fatal. Physiologically, you only die from handgun wounds if you take a central nervous system shot, which is highly unlikely.   Most deaths from handgun wounds are psychological. If you can get ambulance help right away, you'll probably be saved.   No matter what, **Do not** allow yourself to be taken to a secluded area Why! No help there.

Outdoors.   In parks, of course. Rapists attack weaponless joggers running alone and then use bushes. After dark and early mornings are most frequent times.

Public elevators and subterranean parking garages. They wait in the garage and push the call button until they catch a woman alone. In underground parking garages, they hide behind cars and move along with the sound of footsteps as the victim walks. Thus, the victim never sees her attacker. When she slows down to get into her car, they attack.

When alone. You're a much more probable target when all by yourself. As much as you can, go everywhere in pairs. A crowd is even better.

In confined areas. Public elevators are human traps which move vertically between places where no help is available. Avoid elevators when alone. Use stairs. You can run down stairs as fast as anyone, and if attacked from below, you have good kicking advantage.

USING THE DEFCON SYSTEM

Short for Defense Condition, this system tells you how to address a threat in order to get an early first push on the psycho-sexual situation.

At DefCon #1, when a threat is 10 ft. away: Make confident, eye-to-eye contact. It does two things for you. First, It makes you exude confidence---perhaps even bravado. Second, when any perp gets eye-to-eye contact with his intended victim, it makes him feel as if he is identified. Access your weapon or look for something you can use as a weapon. Look for a means of escape. Where there are others nearby, look for temporary allies. Seek out a place where defense will be easier. If it's a stare in your direction you don't like, stare back angrily, defiantly, with the meanest look you can give. **Don't** look away, slouch, or act afraid! That will allow the psycho-sexual situation to move over to the left, and the battle may be lost. Even though rape is most often committed by a loner, check for an accomplice, especially in gang territory.

At DefCon #2, your weapon should be pointed (under cover) at your suspect with the safety off. Watch his face! If he grins, speak first---be strong and tough. With your weapon ready, but hidden (in your purse with your hand on it) command this threat to **buzz off!** Also, you should be moving to safer, perhaps higher, ground.   If you can retreat and get away, do that. If he speaks, put him down right away with a strong, confident and harsh voice.

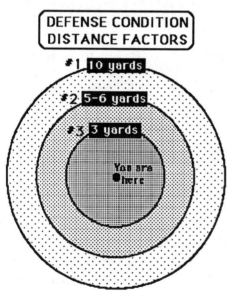

Talk to him in the same tone of voice you would use on a stray dog. Commands such as, "*Get away from me, now! Get lost! Get out of here!*" all serve to stifle his power and control, and convert the psycho-sexual situation in your favor. Once you've announced to a would-be attacker that you're not afraid to shoot, and he continues to approach, you have real reason to fear for your life.

Modern rape includes a long term threat to both mental and physical health (such as STD's---sexually transmitted disease, including AIDS). Therefore, lethal force is right, as well as righteous. Almost everywhere, mortal fear makes a strong case for shooting in self-defense.

Don't let any problem escalate to DefCon #3. Stay alert and ready to strike. We believe: In most major U.S. cities today, if your hand doesn't grasp your weapon in your coat pocket or purse at least twice a month, you aren't paying close enough attention to those around you. We estimate that a majority of female urban dwellers who live in a major city and follow normal activity patterns face a DefCon #1 situation twice a month. Take charge! Identify a serious threat; then give one warning. Once you've warned him to leave you alone and commanded him to go away, with no result, refer him to a higher authority---like his Maker.

Finally, if it gets to DefCon #3 anyway. The threat is close. Note here, of course, that all threats don't sneak up on you in three stages. Most rapists are good at surprise and ambush. They have plenty of time to study the area, and stalking you keeps them on the left (aroused) side of the psycho-sexual circle because they perceive you as helpless and in their power, (even though you may not know it). It's similar to the psycho-sexual situation created by the peeping Tom (with no fear of rejection; no fear of being pushed back on the right).

After you warn your attacker at close range, no more hesitation! The key to success in using a weapon is to get ready long before being confronted. When you do shoot, keep shooting until you're absolutely sure the threat has been neutralized. Putting several rounds into your attacker probably proves how scared you were. Remember to fire one warning shot in the air---your last shot. Witnesses will all be asked, "How many shots did you hear?" If only two are in the perps body and everyone heard three . . . After it's over, answer no questions; let your attorney speak for you.

WHAT TO DO WHEN AMBUSHED
Ambushed?   Counter attack immediately. Overbearing, first-strike counter measures create a psycho-sexual turn off situation. Scream at him with the strongest, most demeaning tone of voice you own. You must convert the psycho-sexual situation to the right side of the diagram. It's time to become 100% physical if you possibly can. All DefCon #3 measures apply.

TAKE KARATE?
I recommend defense classes---but not for self defense because, before you can work your destructive magic, you have to let the danger get too close. Martial fighting techniques—knees to the groin, stomping the vamp of a foot—all require close contact with an enemy normally stronger and more willful.   Think you're strong . . ? Try wrestling with a rapist on drugs. Defense classes help you to develop confidence, which is read like a book by any experienced street thug. Thus, you keep the psycho-sexual situation in your favor.

Will he kill? If you're absolutely sure this rapist is going to kill you if you resist, consider compliance (which is not submission!). **Even in a clinch, however, be constantly alert for an opportunity to counter attack while the enemy is distracted.** If you must comply, report the incident and seek counselling right away.

NON-SHOOTING OFFENSE
Resolve now to fight. Be mentally prepared to the max. "Defense" is a nice euphemism, but the best defense is an overpowering offense. Train, and determine with your full will that if you're attacked, you'll win decisively. If your resolution is firm, it will show and the psycho-sexual situation will initially be in your favor. Dress for battle, not looks. Wear comfortable clothes you can move around in. Footwear needs to give you maneuverability instead of style.

Prepare, train, and determine with your full will that if you're attacked, you'll resist with every bit of strength, knowledge, and resources you have at your disposal. Pre-plan your counter attack now---not by considering weapons---but by first thinking about targets. After that, inventory your weapons, or acquire new ones.

Targets to attack are: The eyes, throat, ear openings, and groin. In *EVERYBODY'S OUTDOOR SURVIVAL GUIDE,* we explained three target groups on the human body. They are: Pain Points, Damage Points, and Lethal Points. Practically anything can be used as a weapon in desperate situations. A rat-tailed comb or any sharp object, a hair pin or a sharpened nail file make good weapons and can be used to attack a would-be rapist. With any sharp object, bring that fist hard up under his arms with an uppercut to puncture the rapist's armpit; fight's over. Hair spray (in the eyes) is a good idea. We also like wasp killer because it shoots out at such a distance. High heels narrowed to a point and capped with a hard rubber by a good cobbler are great, but you have to be able to snap kick.

Your kitchen is an arsenal. Serving forks (sharpen the tips), kitchen knives, frying pans, rolling pins, and sauce pans full of hot soup are all great weapons. As a matter of fact, you can keep a pan of hot water on the stove all day for tea. Just don't use a teapot, and practice throwing the water in your backyard until you get good at hitting a target, which should take less than an hour. You should be able to throw a stream of water about six feet accurately with no problem.

Don't forget the weapons God gave you---teeth, fingernails, elbows, knees and feet. Always aim to strike at a tender spot on your target's body. When at grapple range, don't forget to bite. If you bite off a body part, such as the tip of the nose or an ear lobe, spit it back in his face. Kick repeatedly at his shins, the side of his knee and his groin. (Higher kicking targets are risky because you may over-extend.) Elbow the throat from the front, and his ribs if behind you. Knee the groin; jab hard with stiff fingers so your nails go into his eye sockets. Pain coupled with a strong push to change the psycho-sexual atmosphere to the right half of the circle should get you out of trouble.

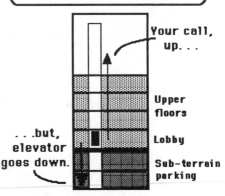

ELEVATORS PROGRAMMED TO ASSIST CRIMINALS IN THE BASEMENTS

Your call, up...

Upper floors

...but, elevator goes down.

Lobby

Sub-terrain parking

ELEVATORS ARE: Small cells travelling up or down in which no help is available. Take stairs.

Report to Authorities? One reason for the increase in rape is this: Not all rapes are reported. Many rape experts disagree with one another on methods of escape, whether or not to submit, etc., but the one thing everyone definitely agrees on is that every rape <u>and attempted rape</u> should be reported to the police. As it stands, less than 10% are reported. We think that's one reason rapists typically try to degrade their victims so severely; it leaves the victim with nothing more than a deep desire to get the incident out of their mind. If I suffered that kind of treatment, would I want to report it? I'm not sure. While the laws and methods we have employed with victims (to protect rapists' constitutional rights) have become less oppressive, reporting a rape still is a frightful thing to do. Easy for me to say, but **reporting is the right thing to do.**

Also, experts agree that victims should seek immediate medical attention. As much as you'll want to, don't clean up or change clothes. You've become a walking inventory of criminal evidence the prosecution will need, and without which, they may be compelled to make a deal. You face a whole series of unpleasant tasks, from gathering evidence, to reliving the experience, to cross examination on a witness stand before a defense attorney.

> The law is swinging back to the conservative side with regard to cross examination of rapist accusers. During an interview with long-time attorney Michael Green in Chula Vista, Ca, he said, "Even if the accuser were a prostitute, it won't be entered into evidence."

Rapists know degrading their victims makes it less likely that a report will be filed, however, and use more trauma and degradation as a means of (further) controlling the victim. If you don't report it, he thinks of himself as cool, and he'll seek out other victims or return to brutalize you one more time, without feeling.

You make your case stronger by reporting the incident immediately, calling a local rape crisis counselor, and allowing all evidence to be gathered with meticulous detail. We apologize for the attitudes you'll encounter in some male police officers, who perhaps have just lost everything in a divorce, or who've become hardened in their attitude because they've seen so many falsely reported.

> ABOUT FALSE REPORTS
> Women who falsely report a rape commit a terrible crime against all other women. "Crying wolf" is one reason true reports don't get the attention they deserve. Because police hear false reports, they sometimes appear to be rude or cold when taking a genuine report.

FIREARMS---THE MORE MEANINGFUL DEFENSE
Buy a handgun, preferably nothing lighter than a .38 Special. Careful, don't buy too much handgun, or you will leave it at home more often than you carry it. Street people will read the confidence in your stature with your hand in your purse on your weapon; you'll avoid a lot of trouble.

Three cautions: A. Never bluff. You won't fool anybody with a lot of criminal experience. B. If you draw your gun at close range, shoot fast; once they grab it successfully, you lose. C. Don't draw without resolve to shoot. Your life is in danger! Promise me now---you will let this rapist find out first hand if there really is---life after death. Don't wound. If you wound or disable an assailant with a firearm, and he survives, he'll take you to court or cause you to be charged with a crime. You won't believe the gentleman's appearance and conduct in court, or the way he will lie about you, the feminazi who shot him. Almost all rapists project their problem onto another person. He will sincerely believe that you were the aggressor and he'll be convincing.

Because wounding a rapist is such a bad idea, you need to use ammunition designed specifically for defense. Think of the innocent people you might hit with standard ammo, which could very well pass easily through your target and whistle into somebody else. Hopefully, this is ammo you will never use, but you can't afford to do an inadequate job of defending yourself. Practice either with this special ammo, or with cheaper ammo that shoots the same, both in bullet weight and velocity, so you can get a feel for how it shoots.

One of the great self-defense lines was delivered by Eli Wallach in the film *The Good, the Bad, and the Ugly*. One of Ugly's early victims with only one arm finds him taking a leisurely bubble bath. With gun drawn, he delivers a long spiel about how he tracked Ugly down and how he would kill him. Ugly shoots him several times with a revolver he'd been holding midst the bubbles in the tub and then delivers this timeless line: "When you gotta shoot, don't talk. Shoot!"

Don't hesitate! Simply draw and fire. The key to success in using any weapon is early preparation. If you shoot, put in a couple of rounds, at least. Keep shooting until you're 100% positive the threat has been neutralized. Permanently! Then reload. Putting several rounds into your attacker might well be used in court by your attorney to show how scared you were.

The bad news is: about one fourth of the women in the U.S. will be attacked by a rapist during their lifetime. The good news is: You can be a member of the other--- untouchable three out of four. You can apply all you've learned here; be perceptive, strong, defiant, maybe even destructive, and convert the psycho-sexual situation to your favor.

Do all of the above; and live your life unscathed.

NOTE ON CALL-OUT BOXES
Call out boxes are intended for recreational reading and provide the reader with a break from the main topic. Although some appreciate the thoughts, others will be incensed. The publisher takes no stand, other than to allow the author's freedom of expression.

PROBABILITY OF FUTURE CRIMES ASSIGNED FOR SENTENCING AND PAROLE.
Every criminal's category (armed robbery, burglary) and history will give a reasonable indication on the likelihood of his future offenses. Similar to insurance actuarial tables, that information can be graphed to give you a likely projection of his future performance in society. Those tables must become a factor in sentencing, parole, and how much victim insurance a convict would be required to purchase. If bad driver's should pay higher insurance rates as assigned risks, how much more should a convict pay?

```
┌─────────────────────────────────────────────────────────────┐
│          COURTS: TAKE JUDICIAL NOTICE OF SIXTH SENSE          │
│     Citizens are not allowed to use more force than that which │
│ they perceive as being used on them.  Key word here is "perceive."  If │
│ the criminal had previous a conviction or a previous arrest, then the │
│ citizen's assessment of danger was correct, and the danger perceived │
│ was real.  Therefore, no crime in shooting a perpetrator.     │
└─────────────────────────────────────────────────────────────┘
```

```
┌─────────────────────────────────────────────────────────────┐
│          THE P A U L (Points Adding Up to Limit) SYSTEM       │
│               FOR CRIMINAL ACCOUNTABILITY.                    │
│     How is it that bad drivers accumulate points for vehicle code │
│ infractions, but a criminal automatically keeps his status as a good │
│ citizen?  If you get four points for speeding 70 mph in a 25 mph │
│ zone, shouldn't a burglar accumulate points too?  How many points │
│ should we assess a violent offender?  A repeat offender?  Couldn't the │
│ court assign points to young criminals?                       │
│     Then, what might be the penalties for an accumulation of  │
│ points on a criminal's record?                                │
│              Loss of welfare, housing allowance, and food stamps. │
│              Loss of right to sue.                            │
│              Loss of aid to dependant's (criminal's) mother.  │
│              Loss of civil rights in criminal codes, i.e., Miranda. │
│              Imprisonment only in a third world foreign country on a │
│ contract basis with visitation over video link-up.           │
│              Loss of access to public lands.                  │
│              Loss of citizenship.                             │
│              Finally, court designation of this individual as an │
│ enemy of the United States, with no rights whatsoever, and the status │
│ of an enemy soldier during wartime.                           │
│                                                               │
│     With such a system in place, criminals would be properly │
│ identified.  Also, no penalty would accrue to a police officer who │
│ became over enthusiastic while suppressing a criminal.  Cops know │
│ bad guys.  Juries have to guess, and our law imposes no status on a │
│ plaintiff with a criminal record who comes into court after being │
│ coached to act like a gentleman.  Thus, crazy lawsuits.  Among many │
│ others, a suit for wrongful death brought by relatives of a deceased │
│ perp who shot a sheriff.                                      │
└─────────────────────────────────────────────────────────────┘
```

Time Magazine reported in Oct 93, just after twelve year old Polly Klas was abducted at knife point from a slumber party in Petaluma California, that 4,500 children are taken every year in the United States. Good God; what have we come to? That's 12 per day.

Chapter 9

How to...
KEEP CHILDREN SAFE AND SECURE

For defense purpose, we define two groups of children—under 12 and teenagers. Both age groups are at risk. Parents often trust other elements of society to provide a safe atmosphere for children, but that trust often leads to disaster. In school for example, our children are exposed to disease, pregnancy, drugs and all kinds of violence.

Listen to Doctor James Dobson, famous for *Focus on The Family,* a talk radio show. With great concern about teenagers, he says, "Just get them through it." That's what we'll help you do with your children. Let's see what we can do to help your child stay alive and unmolested long enough to get through it and become an adult.

Telling your child not to talk to "<u>strangers</u>" can be improved upon, because little children think of "<u>strangers</u>" as sort of a monster. Tell you child: Avoid contact with, or speaking to, "<u>anyone you don't know</u>."

Scene: Nicely dressed pedophile (actor) with picture of puppy goes to playground. He successfully convinced several children into helping him look for his puppy, and they followed him away from the playground.

Let's focus on the little ones. In Oct 93, *Time Magazine* reported that child abduction by a stranger takes place 12 times a day. NCMEC, the National Center for Missing and Exploited Children, confirms that figure, and adds that 72% of the victims are female. Get immediate help if your child is abducted by calling NCMEC at **1-800-THE-LOST,** or 1-800-843-5678. Also get involved; call that number if you see a child who looks like a picture on your milk carton or a poster.

To help prevent abduction by a non-custodial parent, take a photo of you and your child. If you have one, include a photo of the other parent. In a local copy shop, make several of these pictures along with a letter something like the following:

"I'm sorry to inform you that Daniel's father (mother) and I divorced. The court awarded custody to me. His father (mother) is **not** to pick the child up from your institution. All visitation and other contact will be handled by me, personally, from the home only."

ABDUCTION BY STRANGER
Over 75% of pedophiles are male about 31 years old. People will say of him, "Gee—the kids just loved him." Kids are often convenient victims; they're available; they can't fight back, and they don't have a disease. Perhaps any young child for whom he can be the first and only lover will create the thrill he seeks. Today, teachers, clergy, family members and older students all potentially add to the threats our children face. Our children are no longer safe in their schools, in church, in their neighborhoods, or even their own homes. Therefore: **You must be always on guard.** If there is crime for which all-out war is required, it has to be assault against children. But we can't always be with them. Worse, sometimes they simply disappear. If they do, **immediate response while the trail is hot** is the best course of action. For that reason, we developed the **CRS.**

CRS CHILD RECOVERY SYSTEM

Prepare now to get help finding your lost child. **Have current photographs made.** (Three months old, maximum.) You need a close facial shot, a stand-up photo near some kind of car (to convey a sense of height), and a separate shot of any birthmarks or scars. This next step is critical: Take these photos to a copy shop (Kinko's) or photo house and **have them half-toned**. Put them in an envelope; carry them with you.

Now, write a brochure. Type it out or print it off your computer in large, 14 pt. type or bigger. Leave space for photos. On top, write: **ABDUCTED CHILD!**, followed immediately by space for a hand-printed date and time. Then write, "answers to the name, Tykie." If a stranger calls out the child's nickname, the abductor wouldn't know, but the child may turn her head---bingo! On the rest of the brochure, place a business phone number and an address where anyone can write or call. If you can make financial arrangements, post a reward in your brochure. Even $200 will be enough to make a lot of people stop and help you recover your child.

IN A SITUATION WHERE THE CHILD DISAPPEARS IN AN *ENCLOSED AREA

Here are the immediate recovery procedures: Ask security to announce, "Ladies and gentlemen, parents and their daughter have become temporarily separated. As a courtesy, _____ will now close all exits to all children for eight minutes." Immediately, security puts half toned photos and your typed material together to make a hundred copies of your child's flyer, which go to every exit, security person and cashier. The photos---closeup facial, child standing in front of door, plus prominent scars will help keep that child from being taken out of that enclosed area.

CHILD SECURITY IN CROWDED PLACES

Of lesser importance, set your child for sound.   With their voices only, they can't call very far.   But with a whistle, they can be heard over a long range.   Outdoors for example, a whistle blow will carry downwind for miles.

Teach your child what makes a sound carry.   An open door out of a tiled restroom during a whistle blast can be heard by the whole department store.   Outdoors, a rock canyon will broadcast everywhere below.   On a city street between tall buildings, a blast will alert everyone on the block.   Buy several whistles for your child.   Attach a backup whistle to his tennis shoe strings.   Have your child blow the whistle around the home so you learn exactly the way it sounds and how much volume she produces.

OTHER THINGS TO DO

Make sure your children can give the "911" operator their name, address and phone number.   Volunteer hunter-safety instructors teach new hunters to stay in one place when lost in the woods.   The same applies to children when lost in public areas. They need to stay put.   Within a short time, their parent, baby-sitter, or teacher will discover who's missing and return to the last place they were together.

Strange cars have to be identified and avoided much the same as strange people.   Teach them to avoid all contact and speak only to a **uniformed** police officer, security guard, or store employee.   As you go around with your child, point these people out and ask the child to identify them. If someone other than a uniformed police officer accosts them, teach your children to make a hell of a fuss, draw attention to themselves, and cry out "kidnap" for help.   Screaming "Help; this is not my parent!" works well.   Almost all child abductors succeed by beguiling the child with a variety of clever ploys. "Please, help me find my puppy!" (Shows photo). "Could you help me find an address?" "Mommy needs help and sent me to get you."

Trick commonly employed by pedophiles: Show the child a badge, (sold by mail order), tell him you're a cop, and order him to come along. The child simply walks off and you never see him or her again.

Instruction to your child: Stay put! Never walk off with anybody for any reason! Tell lots of adults around you in a loud voice, **"I don't know this man; please help me."**

If lost or in trouble, there is a hierarchy of help your child should learn. First, a man or woman in police uniform. Second, an older, well-dressed couple. They come from a generation in which clean and decent conduct, respect for property, and love of little children was common. Third, women are more loving and caring towards little children as a matter of instinct. Avoid scruffy-looking people. Note this: People who abduct children come in all forms and manners of grooming. Scruffy looks do **not** mean a person is an abductor. Teach your child to trust nobody, and focus on the 31 year old male as particularly dangerous.

Part of the reason for these crimes is the allure and desirability of the innocence of children. During breakfast with a confirmed pedophile who lived in the Philippines and could therefore pursue his interest freely, he became enthusiastic as he shared his excitement with me, "Because they're sweet; they love only me; they're gorgeous and they're pure." In the US, the illegality adds to the fantasy.

The same threats our children face today will also face them as adults. Thus, teaching them to avoid or to deal with these threats in our absence is our major concern. Watch your attitudes. Make your children cautious, but not terrified. Terror leads to panic. Panic is a child's worst enemy. Training is the key, and it has long-term value. As the threats change, new sources of danger are discovered. Simply adjust and build on previous lessons.

HIRING A FOUR-LEGGED BODY GUARD

Prior to the time your child starts school, see if you can get him interested in a puppy. If your child mistreats animals, this won't work. On the other hand, if you can teach your child to take good care of the dog, the benefits are tremendous. You'll get a full time bodyguard who can sense dangerous situations, run faster than you'll ever hope to, attack ferociously and bite unbelievably hard if your child is faced with peril. Dogs often bite people who raise a hand to hit their buddy, a child. Also, dogs can smell a wrong person long before humans get the message.

The breed will be personal opinion. While any dog will do, we find the mixed breeds to be best. They're not inbred and therefore more stable and healthier. Also, spayed females are better than males; they don't get distracted. Working dogs, part shepherds are fine. They've been bred for the purpose of watching over sheep and goats. They herd them. With children, they often perform magnificently. We've heard stories of dogs who refused to let a father spank a child. One Australian shepherd we know comes alive at 2:45 because Sally comes home from school. He waits at the bus stop.

Don't let your child handle any of the puppy's discipline. But, do have the child take care of the puppy, play with it, feed it and nurture it as much as possible. If the puppy comes to your home when the child is four, he'll be the child's best friend by age five, and you should get an excellent 10 years of top-quality guard service.

Even with a good dog, don't rely on the animal. All of the training you do for your children and the time you spend watching them needs to be done as if the dog didn't exist---with one exception---training the dog to find your child on command*. Still, if you ever slip up, the extra guard on full time duty can be worth more than all the expense and inconvenience a dog represents.

*I trained my Weimaraner to find my children on command. We played games at night. The kids hid while I held the dog, then let it go to locate them. The dog never lost!

THINGS TO AVOID

It used to be desirable to dress your child as well as you could afford. Not anymore---especially in some public schools. We've documented stories of children who were shot by a schoolmate because they wouldn't give up their expensive shoes or a nice jacket. Children from different parts of your city and entirely different family backgrounds may have vastly different values. If your child is forced to go to school with other children who're looking for a way to earn some respect, your well dressed child is at risk.

Sack lunches made at home are a good idea. In some schools, kids make a good living robbing lunch money from other students. They threaten their victims with a severe gang beating if the child tells. For years on end they collect a dollar a day from several victims and your child spends his academic years in terror.

TRAINING CHILDREN

Young children need preventative defense training more than anyone else because they're defenseless. They can't go armed. Teach them to avoid or escape from danger, rather than how to face it and fight against it. To fully understand the concept of training for a particular mission (in your child's case: staying unmolested and alive), training needs a clearly defined objective (read General Schwartzkopf's biography). So you begin teaching your children the reasons for the training. Then, conduct a field training exercise. It's like a game. You set up hypothetical situations and teach the child how to evade and escape. Long trips in a car are a good time to do this. Children are especially afraid of the dark. Conduct your training first during the day, then dusk, then after dark. Be careful **not** to create a fearful training experience.

As soon as you feel your child comprehends instructions, and the reasons behind them, it's time to start his or her defense training. When children begin to accept responsibility, you need to involve them in family defense planning. Start with warnings.

Identify the various child-dangers and list the threats which apply to each area. Added to the standard, ". . . don't play with matches," expand the list of warnings to include a few more examples of the threats they may face. Be careful not to terrify the child. He or she needs to be concerned, not paralyzed by fear.

Explain the purpose of the safe room or sanctuary as well as the Inner Sanctum to your children. Show your children how you want them to approach the safe room (crawl or run) during the night if you call them. Have them practice this approach several times. Just as schools conduct regular fire drills, conduct security drills.

Teach all children to come to the safe room in your house if they encounter trouble. No matter what the problem, comfort the child in the safe room. Little Betty skins her knee and comes to you crying. Carry her to the safe room, comfort her, clean and dress the wound, no matter how slight, and when she is feeling better, tell her how safe she is in that room with you. Never discipline a child in that room. You want the child to associate that room with security and safety.

ANSWERING THE DOOR AT HOME. **NEVER!**

Whether or not your home is posted with a sign discouraging unknown visitors, **don't** allow your children to open any door at any time for visitors. Of course, kids are easier to fool than adults, especially if they've been taught to respect elders. Furthermore, they make easy to capture and detain hostages.

TELEPHONE PROCEDURES

<u>Children</u>: Don't answer the phone and give any information <u>of any kind</u> to anyone. Not your name, age, grade---absolutely nothing. Don't give out your address, where you go to school, whether or not you walk or ride, what kind of car your daddy drives—nothing.

<u>Being accosted by any stranger, either in public or at home</u>. Regarding strangers, teach your children to distrust nice-ness. Abductors seldom appear to be mean; most have developed a candy-coated approach to an art form. Shepherd dogs are helpful with "nice" strangers; they seem to sense who's genuine and who's not.

Being sexually molested by suggestion, touch, or request from anyone, including family members, and friends of family, and others who supposedly are in authority, requires the child to report it <u>immediately</u>. Many cases of child abuse or molestation go unreported by the victims because children believe adults can do no wrong. Let your kids know that teachers, baby-sitters, other adults and family members can do terribly wrong things. We believe it's best to teach this: "<u>Your body is a sacred temple given to you by God. Nobody has a right to invade it.</u>"

Children often fear reporting an adult or worry about not being believed if they tell on an adult. They're sometimes willing to take abuse, suffer pain and humiliation for years, rather than risk trouble for saying something bad about an adult, especially an authority figure. Children often sense the advances are wrong, but they don't want to cause harm to the abuser or destroy a loving relationship. Your children need to trust that you will always take their side on this problem.

Let your child's teachers and other school staff know about your children's training. If a problem teacher knows your children are not afraid to tell, that teacher will most likely choose another victim. Moreover, teachers involved in the same kinds of pursuit know and talk to one another. Once they hear about your closeness and training, your child will be off-limits to sexual abusers at school.

Parents, be aware of strange people or strange vehicles in your neighborhood. Any time you see one, make a record of the license number, the make and model and year of the car, and try to get a description of the occupant. Children should learn to do the same; you can make a game out of it. If a car you suspect has bent or damaged or unreadable plates, react quickly and positively. You're never wrong to call a suspicious car into police headquarters.

Fingerprint your children. Keep copies of birth certificates, social security cards and passports in a safe deposit box. Also, starting with a child who is an infant, put together a dossier and add to it as the years pass. Photographs, likes and dislikes, fears, memory keys, speech pattern peculiarities, a five-to-ten minute audio or video of the child at play and in conversation. Make sure to get facial close-ups and pay particular attention to special marks, scars, dental configurations, and ears. Store all this safely. Many parents fail to photograph children on a regular basis because they don't realize the child is growing and changing. Make a rule: New photos at least every three months. Also, take special photos for special occasions involving a costume, such as Halloween. If your child disappears, you need a recent photo and you need it now, both in costume and in regular dress.

The latest development in this crime is rapid transfer of information by computer. With a recent photo, you can have computer hackers, police departments and other agencies furnished with a photo within a few hours, **but you must have a recent photograph!**

Also, make a list of special things only your child would remember or be familiar with. For example, what funny thing happened on her tenth birthday, something special about you or your spouse they will be sure to remember, a favorite toy or pet, or a secret place. All of this helps authorities and private detectives identify missing children, even after years have elapsed.

ALWAYS REMEMBER . . .

What was your child wearing? Do you always carry a couple of current pictures with you in case she or he gets lost? Do not put name tags on your children. Pedophiles will call them by name, then convince them to walk away because, "Mommy sent me to get you and bring you to her."

WILL YOUR CHILD GO SOMEWHERE ALONE?

It's not a good idea to allow your child to go on a trip (even supervised) until the child is trained in Escape and Evasion. This is a subject taught to all military members when the possibility of their capture exists. Could your child be captured? The germs took 4,500 prisoners last year. Most children don't have a clue how to escape. Fix that.

First, acclimate the child to darkness. Almost all children are afraid of the dark, and it takes a lot of training to counteract what seems to be natural---fear of the dark. But with that fear conquered, the child could learn to use the night as an ally. Consider the life cycle of the abductor. Often, they're addicted to drugs and alcohol, which means they sleep heavily. If your child is secure in darkness because of all your night training and she knows how to evade and hide, chances of escaping are excellent.

Be careful with this training. **Do not** scare your child. To bring them up so they are competent at night, each training experience must be positive. If something goes wrong, you'll reinforce fear and ruin any hopes of making the child operationally proficient in darkness.

Little Shirely's daddy would often send his daughter out into the night---into a shed full of spider webs to retrieve some item. Some 25 years later, she still has fear of spiders and has difficulty coping with darkness.

So take the child on walks in absolutely dark places. Make sure where you go is safe, otherwise you'll be somewhat afraid and the child will catch this. (Dobson: "Value systems are not taught to a child; they are caught by the child.") Hold his or her hand. Make the child feel secure. As soon as the child becomes somewhat bold in the dark, play hide and seek. Get another child to play with you, because you want the two to hide in the same place (to give them a feeling of security.) You're always it.

If you want to win all the time, bring your dog. Reward the dog lavishly when he finds the child. Why? Suppose you lose your child in a crowd. You can turn your dog loose with a "find Emily" command, and the dog will track the scent. When searching for your child during a game, such as hide and seek, they'll be easy to find at first because they might make noise, or their bright clothing will be easy for you to see in the dark. But as time goes on, they can improve. They'll get better at night when they learn the following:

NOISE DISCIPLINE AND CAMOUFLAGE
The child needs to learn what clothes can't be seen in the dark, and how not to make any noise. If the child wears white sneakers, teach him or her how to cover them. Teach the child how to wash his or her face and the backs of hands in dirt so no skin surfaces shine and reflect light. Also, the child needs to learn three valuable tricks: a. never stare at ar pursuer, and, b., don't move; stay perfectly still, and finally c. looking quickly at both sides of a person in pitch dark enables the child to use night vision to see better.

Almost all humans have a sixth sense, and will stare back in the direction from which they are stared at. If you don't believe this, look at the driver in the car next to you at a stop light. For no apparent reason, many will turn and look at you. When a pervert is looking for a child, he will be drawn to the area from which the child stares at him. Also, peripheral vision always picks up movement. Even though the kidnapper isn't looking directly at the place where your child is hiding, the slightest movement off to the side can cause discovery.

Finally, teach your child to go into places where his or her small size will fit, but where big people cannot. Even with the kidnapper a few feet away, the youngster can drop down and roll under a car where she or he can't be reached. Play a game (Field Training Exercise). You be the kidnapper. Tell your child to try and get away from you. One day, you'll be walking through a parking lot and the child will disappear because she dropped to the ground and rolled under a car. Try as you might, you won't be able to reach her. She can watch your feet, and whenever you run around the car, she can move to the opposite side.

GOING TO A FOREIGN COUNTRY
Very little can cause more panic than losing one of your children in a foreign country. Directions in a foreign land are always confusing; the language barrier becomes a terrifying problem, and the police seem not to be interested.

When you take your children overseas, always take a certified copy of their birth certificate along. It's also a good idea to get a passport for all of your children, even toddlers. Bring extra passport photos with you, too. Here, however, you want to half-tone the photos and make copies with you **before** you travel. Lots of third world countries don't have the copy facilities we do, and the wait could enable a kidnapper to get away. Remember, you want to get your child's picture all over immediately after loss.

Pay close attention to their whereabouts, and make them pay close attention to yours. The rule is; Never out of daddy's or mommy's sight. Of course, you do the same. Don't turn your back. Teach them to walk ahead of you so you can survey the area constantly.

139

Think about what to do if your child gets lost in a foreign country. In Mexico, for example, where could he go to meet you? Here's one plan: Type up a note in Spanish (pay to have it done) which says. "This child is a son or daughter of a U.S. police officer. Please take this child directly to Hotel Palacio and collect a ____peso reward from the desk." Make arrangements at the desk so they know to advance the money for the child's return. Place the note in the child's shoe. Train the child to give the note **only** to a police officer. Cab drivers could be trouble with a note like that if they think of a greater reward.

UPGRADING THEIR TRAINING

As your children mature they should become more and more a part of the family defenses. Keep on training as long as your children live at home. Upon reaching the age when handgun training will be available to them, teach safety and basics; then let them begin to shoot small caliber handguns. Games in the house played with all the lights out and the shades drawn help lessen children's fear of the dark. Night training is important because that's when most criminal activity takes place. If your child learns to maneuver noiselessly in the dark with camouflage, she can escape anybody easily. As soon as they're able, teach them how and when to use the defense weapons in the family arsenal. Make them familiar with the alarm system and your security lighting system.

Teach your children to keep secrets. In that category will be: family valuables, travel plans and any personal information. All that information is classified a "secret." Nobody outside the family should ever hear about it.

Children's house guests can be a problem. Get to know the parents of your children's' friends. It's best if your child plays with others of similar values and backgrounds. If a "friend" of your child comes around about whom you have a bad feeling, **don't** allow them to hang out together.

TEENAGE CRIME. WHY?

As children grow, chances of losing them to abductors lessen, but other new threats will pose problems. Early training helps them a lot because---even though a threat is one never before faced, the attitude and mindset you gave your child in early years will help. Why so much teenage crime, though? Partly because teens can get away with it; our justice system doesn't punish youngsters, who then grow up with a criminal self image and a taste for evil. Partly because so many teens don't come from two-parent families; perhaps a single mother loves, but seldom restrains with a heavy hand.

If you want to think about it philosophically, consider what would happen in any part of the world where humans with different backgrounds, values, and religions share common space. In early America, you could do a great job of educating students---in one schoolhouse with a chalkboard slate. Why? Everybody had the same or similar values, such as hard work, diligence, respect for elders.

In modern times, we think we have a better idea. Our schools are multi-million dollar educational facilities and we dedicate them. Ironically, we can't get the students dedicated. The counter-productive cloud of rebellion is ever present. Peer pressure against academic achievement and for sex and drugs reigns. Juvenile exemptions for crimes encourage evil. Weapons are everywhere and upgraded. Under circumstances this bad, some teachers have an alcohol problem or take drugs, themselves.

CLOTHING TO AVOID TROUBLE

Teach your children to go into social situations (school) with a fresh, decent, clean-cut appearance. Otherwise, they might feel a need to follow the crowd for whom they dress. In addition to style, watch the cost. Some shoes, jackets and jewelry cost a lot, and could encourage armed robbery or assault. Leave expensive clothes at home. Dressed nicely, she or he will find other companions in similar styles. As parents, watch and enforce your dress code. It will help.

Teenage criminal perpetrators victimize those with whom they normally come in contact. Witness victims who die between the ages of 18 and 24. Who shoots? Same peer group. Of course, one way to avoid violence is not to associate with people who carry weapons in school. Cars fall into the same category as clothing. If the car will draw a lot of bad companions around your teenager, don't buy it. Expensive cars are advertisements at school. They announce: My family has money; burglarize us!

Brian talked about his mother's BMW because it was cool. So, somebody at school stole his keys. At 3:00 in the morning, the car disappeared; the police found it wrecked. What if the thieves had been stopped by police? With the keys, they could have claimed the car was a loan.

Fighting used to be something some parents taught their children and encouraged them to do. While it's important to teach a child there is a time---when all other options have been explored---make sure it doesn't happen often or for no severe reason. School fights today often mean severe beatings or knifings to the loser. If your son or daughter wins a fight, it could lead to fatal retaliation.

TEEN RAPE
In some areas, 30% of teen girls become pregnant, either by rape or persuasion. Here's the problem: Many boys view rape as nothing more than extra persuasion. The street philosophy of, "anything you're not strong enough to keep belongs to me," has also fostered another kind of rape---where a male is a victim of another male.

Not only does a daughter have to avoid situations where rape might occur, but she has to be extremely careful whom she dates. Encourage <u>double dating</u>. If your daughter spends time alone with a young man, even though innocent, he'll be severely pressured to brag to his friends in a locker room that he made it, went all the way.

Once that story gets around, she's rapeable. Many teen rapists feel that if the victim did it with others, he's should get his fair share. Sex with her is a way of bringing himself on a par with his peers. (Again, the rite of passage.) Also, kids do know that an attorney will pound on the girl's past if she charges rape. Some boy's have been known to solicit false testimony from locker room friends even *before* they make contact with your daughter. With even a shred of past indecent behaviour on her part, she could become a target for rape.

The best prevention here is caring parents who watch carefully the choice of companions, both male **and** <u>female</u>. Listen to Bill Gothard, from *Basic Youth Conflicts,* "<u>Fathers,</u> you need to interview all of your daughter's prospective dates. All boys know that if the father doesn't care and is unconcerned, they can get away with almost anything?"

Girl friends who are promiscuous will introduce your daughter to boys who expect sexual favors. While your daughter's companions might put on a great front, look for telltale signs such as provocative dress, foul language, jokes about sex, and a family background with a lack of paternal guidance and love. When your daughter's friend mentions that, "My father never comes to see me," watch out. Girls without paternal love seek it out—-frequently with older, more experienced males. Of course—-they'll take your daughter along. In some cases, unsuspecting girls introduced through girlfriends to parties have been gang-raped. You can't be too careful. (*Sally Jesse Raphael Show*, 24 Jan 94. Transcript available from Burrell. Guests: Several rape victims; one victim's father in jail after shooting perpetrator.)

SEXUAL ASSAULT FROM A STRANGER

A whole group of sexual molesters prey on teenagers. The perp enjoys making the young teenager feel guilty. The more guilt the victim feels, the safer the perp feels from report, much less, prosecution.

Most perps know that an increased degree of submission will create more guilt, accompanied by a block in memory and a severe inclination not to tell anybody what happened. Therefore, they force their victims to do despicable acts.

More than any other, this is trouble to avoid. Young teens can be lured into dangerous situations through all kinds of ads for employment. Ads for models, baby-sitters, and private help at home could all be trouble. Parents, you need to check them out very carefully. How? Get Better Business Bureau references. Talk to parents of other clients. Be happy to employ and pay 10% to a legitimate modeling agent with a history in the community for creating wholesome work. Men: **Do not interview prospective baby sitters in your home alone!** If you absolutely must do that, tape the interview covertly. Otherwise, you may find yourself the target of a healthy lawsuit by an irate parent who will try and make the world believe you're a molester.

SEXUAL ASSAULT FROM FAMILY MEMBER

Crisis centers report that many calls came from teenage girls who had been assaulted by a stepparent, an older stepbrother, an uncle, or in some cases, the girl's own father.

> As a phone counselor for a church, I personally heard this: A 14 year old girl had been viciously assaulted by her mother's boyfriend. She had run away from home and was destitute. We called the girl's mother and pleaded with her to take care of her daughter. She refused to believe her boyfriend had committed the crime. Finally, though, she broke down and cried out, "Do you know how hard it is for me to find a boyfriend?"

Mothers who remarry. Your job now is to take good care of your daughter. Watch for signs of trouble. Scripture says,"what comes out of the mouth is in the heart." A leering glance or an off-color remark are sure signs. Trouble can begin with a daughter as young as infancy. Frequent stepfather-daughter excursions away from home or extraordinary nervousness on the young girl's part can be indications. Child molestation is like cancer—better healed if caught early—best healed if cut out completely.

Be careful, of course, where you go for help. Some state organizations are coldly bureaucratic. Therefore, some mothers live in denial and refuse to believe children who report trouble. But if the husband has a problem with lust, you'll want to save your daughter, so act early.

Secrets in a family can be destructive, mothers and daughters are far better off to form a faction against abuse than to ignore the problem. When abuse is unchecked, the daughter will live in degradation and fear. As we're learning today, the psychological damage is devastating and long-lasting. Women abused in childhood have a very difficult time adjusting to married life, and, as with men, often become abusive themselves.

THEFT BY TEENAGERS
Take your children with you. If you leave kids at home, they may have friends over. Innocent fun can get out of hand easily. What would happen if a teenager drank your liquor, became totally drunk, and injured someone. Would you be sued? Might you be liable? What if someone gets hurt in your home during your absence? Also, some of the young people who visit your home may rob it during the visit---and return later for more generous portions.

How could that happen? A percentage of the students in almost every school use crack cocaine. The

145

addiction is all-consuming. All your child has to do is make a mistake and invite one of them to your home, or let one of them crash the party—-and for months thereafter, your house will be a target. If you want to experience some compulsive theft, invite a teen on crack to your party.

This is one of the worst times in the history of our country as far as danger to our children is concerned. Pedophiles are a constant threat. Perverts want to steal and kill them. Peers want to rip them off, and some peers will kill for the shoes or jackets they wear. The most treacherous threat---random violence---is also the most difficult to predict or defend.

If you stay physically close to them, you can prevent most bad things from happening. Once you develop a tight emotional relationship with your child, you can relax in an atmosphere of mutual trust. As the child grows older and leaves the nest more often, you can check up constantly on his or her companions and provide extra steerage through a channel of high morality and good values.

If all goes well, you'll be able to sit back in your golden years, visit your grandchildren---and begin to worry all over again.

CRIME, AND THE LEGISLATURE'S APPROACH
Legislators keep making laws which give criminals a decided advantage. Why? The lawmakers fail to find out who obeys their laws and who doesn't. Good citizens want to live in an orderly society and they obey. A gangbanger could care less. Even if he or she gets caught with an illegal weapon, the charge is seldom added because the prosecutor is dealing with serious crime anyway. The added weapons charge would be a joke.

What is this bad and bitter attitude I hear on the streets about politicians? Many of these people have been victims. Combined, this is their statement: "My country (city, state) has become a toilet, and politicians are the attendants."

CHAPTER 10

FIREARMS FOR PERSONAL DEFENSE

In our opinion, the current rise in crime is only the tip of the iceberg; we're going to see a lot more. Criminals see themselves as free to do anything they want. However, a low self image keeps them imprisoned by the fear of peer disapproval. In their subculture, rebels are heroes; law abiders are losers.

What if a criminal gets caught? Our criminal justice system protects and aids criminals. One example: Mass releases from prisons as urged by the ACLU due to overcrowding. Today's violent criminals are well armed. Often, their weapons are superior to what police carry. If you want to survive, you'll have to learn to be your own bodyguard.

How good a bodyguard can you be? You can study edged weapons and become a master of martial arts. You can carry all kinds of whistles and alarms. But in the streets, only one defensive weapon out-performs all others---that's a firearm.

Don't buy a gun for defense if you won't train with it; lack of training can make a firearm a personal liability rather than an asset. Make sure the weapons in your home are secured. Theft of a weapon often creates future problems for many innocent people.

Follow these rules:

1. Self defense is no poker game. Street hoods will know you're bluffing. Never pick up a gun unless you mean business---the most serious kind.

2. Do everything you can to avoid serious problems. Never expose yourself to danger. Take no risks. Let the dog bite, the alarm go off, or the tear gas spray before you go to guns. This is a weapon of last resort, and you need to define your own personal limit of abuse before you go to this defense measure.

3. Have **nothing** to do with alcohol or drugs where guns are kept.

4. Make sure you shoot in self defense. <u>Even though you know you were right</u>, follow all the precautions we lay out in Chapter 12, called, *After the Attack.*

Assuming you follow the above rules, disregard the gun control sentiment in this country and acquire a firearm. Learn to use it, carry it with you everywhere, learn to maintain it, and practice regularly. Otherwise, you may as well put your name in early to get a reservation on somebody's victim list.

Many citizens confuse right with righteous. We all know our own hearts and therefore make the mistake of thinking our criminal justice system will judge us accordingly. Don't be fooled. Many an intended victim acting in defense went to jail because they acted righteously and then, failed to take precautions afterwards the same way a criminal would to avoid arrest and trouble. Let God be your only judge. Avoid the law, enacted by men who too frequently are drunkards, bribe takers and other kinds of criminals, themselves. Can we trust a system they created?

GUN? WHAT KIND?

The options are practically unlimited. Firearms are available in every size, shape and finish you can imagine. You can choose from pump, semi-auto, or double barrel shotguns. Handguns come in small, medium, or large. Guns can be blued, nickel plated or stainless steel. In addition to all the finishes, steels, barrel lengths and sizes, you have to tackle the major problem, namely, which caliber or gauge and which type of weapon to choose.

HANDGUNS

Low power handguns (such as 22's, 25's, and 32's) don't provide sufficient power to insure clean kills, even with multiple hits. The high power offerings are harder to control, (recoil) make a quick second shot more difficult, and pose potential danger if they punch through walls and into another room or building.

Granted, it's confusing, but we can simplify the choice. Generally, cartridges are designated by bullet diameter. The period you see in front of the number is a decimal point. So, a .25 caliber bullet is one quarter of an inch in diameter, and a .45 is almost a half.

Ruger makes this **SP-101** double-action trouble free revolver.

Magnum generally means a larger case capacity, and therefore, more powder pushing the bullet faster. The recoil is greater, too. That's why magnum pistols are usually heavier; more metal keeps the gun from blowing apart under the higher pressures developed by these heavier loads.

You can improve on the best factory offering with specialty performance accessories. For about $20, get Uncle Mike's grips with finger-grooves to help hold the weapon on target and absorb recoil. Spend extra bucks on serious go-to-war cartridges so your handgun is more effective.

To save you some reading and reduce confusion, let's get to the point. Then we can discuss all the alternatives, bullet weights, stopping powers, probable shooting ranges, etc. For a quick answer applicable to over 80% of gun buyers, however, <u>this is what to buy:</u> If you're, under 5'-6" (145#'s) and of average strength, you purchase a .38 Special, double action revolver with a four- inch (or less) barrel. If you're over 5'-10" and strong, you can consider a .357 magnum. What's most important in your choice is to make sure the pistol fits you as a shooter, fits in the pocket of your sweat pants or jogging suit, and doesn't make your purse or evening bag feel like a boat anchor dragging on your shoulder. Before you buy, ask a gun dealer to tell you what your intended purchase weighs fully loaded. Then try a weight that heavy in your purse.

Light weight .38's are fine. I'm particularly fond of the new, SP101 <u>stainless</u>, five-shot, double action revolver by Ruger, who has a unique knack for coming up with the perfect product. New metal technology and super design make this a strong <u>lightweight</u> pistol. Of course, the lighter the weapon, the more it will recoil.

If you're a male, over 5'-6" and reasonably strong, purchase a .357 magnum double action revolver with a four-inch (or less) barrel. You don't have to shoot .357's in this weapon all the time; you can load it with .38 Specials for practice. But the .357 pushes a .38 caliber projectile about 300 miles an hour faster (about 500 feet per second) than the Special, which means it will produce more energy and deliver greater penetration.

Buy stainless steel unless you like maintenance. It's not that you don't have to keep stainless clean and lubed. But sweat on a blued weapon will cause rust quickly.

Do you need glasses to read? Then install a different sighting system. Perhaps you can afford to install $180 dollars worth of laser red dot. These sights help make sure you stay on target as you squeeze the trigger. Also, here's a great way to go at greatly reduced expense: Purchase a squeeze bottle of glow-in-the-dark paste and put a line down the top of the barrel (on top of the rib) so you can see your line of fire in the dark. Once you line up the barrel with your target, the only misses you have to worry about will be high or low.

SURE FIRE
THE BATERY POWERED
PISTOL SIGHT

Laser Sight Dot on target. Just hold it there 'n squeeze.

> Lasers are fine, especially for night shooting. But, when your battery goes dead, you have a problem.

HOW TO BUY

Of course, stores specializing in firearms sales are fine. You buy the weapon, write "no" several times on federal forms, wait for whatever time your state requires, and pick up your gun. The weapon is registered to you. Do that---you'll consider yourself a law abiding citizen.

Criminals, even when they buy, go a completely different route. They buy from acquaintances, car trunks, gun shows, swap meets and flea markets. No record is made of the purchase. A stolen weapon is registered to the person from whom it was stolen. No computer or official knows who has possession of that gun. When it winds up with no fingerprints on it in a dumpster or in a lake or river after having killed some body, they could link the fatal bullet to the gun if it were found, but the gun can't be traced to any person especially the shooter who never registered it.

Are used guns OK? Generally, yes. It's hard to screw up a revolver. If you buy at a gun show, you'll easily find several gunsmiths who will give you an inexpensive opinion. You can make a deposit (by check, marked "holding deposit for firearms inspection") in a pawnshop and take the gun to any gun store for an opinion. They have books on used gun value, and the store gunsmith will tell you in a matter of minutes if it's functional. The question you need to answer most concerns, dependability.

> "The gun control laws are stupid!" G. Gordon Liddy, spoken to Don when he was a guest on Liddy's radio show, 16 Aug 93.

As a good citizen, pay for all your firearms purchases by check or credit card and write the serial number of the weapon down so you (only you) have a permanent record of the purchase. If you buy from a gun dealer, he'll make sure you follow the proper procedures for firearms purchase in your state. Then the state has a permanent record of your purchase. If you want to make sure your firearm is not stolen, ask your local police contact to run the serial number through NCIC (National Crime Information Center) to make sure.

A handgun without a comfortable way to carry it is a burden you'll soon want to avoid. Buy good holsters. Several companies now offer load bearing vests for combat, carrying bags for weapons and accessories, and nylon holsters. Built for comfort and easy access, they allow you to carry your weapon with you at all times, including those times when you won't be carrying a handbag. Without good holsters, it just isn't always practical for you to carry a handgun. Since criminals (much in favor of gun control) like to attack when you're <u>not</u> carrying, and the new holsters allow you to carry almost everywhere, you increase your odds of surviving potential crime attacks dramatically. In warm tropical climates, you can use an ankle holster, or perhaps a shoulder holster under your Hawaiian shirt. You can get shoulder holders with vertical, angle and side pulls so you get easy access to your handgun the way you like best. The new holsters allow you to carry your handgun <u>with you</u> rather than leave it at home or in your vehicle.

Likewise, get handy carriers for spare ammunition---either a speed loader (revolver) or a spare magazine. Buy a gun cleaning kit. Better than one for each caliber, get an all-purpose kit. Also, get some lead remover because practice rounds tend to leave lead deposits.

What you've read so far will probably give you enough information to purchase a defense handgun. Though we could fill a book with information and gun facts, (and we did in *Great Livin' in Grubby Times*) let's mention a few more important points you'll need to consider.

Semi-automatic pistols are flatter than revolvers and therefore don't bulge on your body. Think concealment. They also hold more ammo. Many come in a heavier caliber with more stopping power than the .38 Special. But, they can be like spouses; they require tender loving care if you want them to be faithful. Otherwise, they can fail when you need them most. Most home defense shooting confrontations are settled with one shot. So you need a weapon that works—every time! You don't generally need a 50 round drum magazine or "the most powerful handgun in the world." You need a weapon you can use effectively under the most stressful circumstances. For all of the above reasons, we vote for revolver. Double action revolvers are safe and sure.

> The longer the barrel on a pistol, the more accurately it will shoot at a distance. But, the easier it will be for somebody close to take it away from you, and the tougher it will be to conceal. Stay under 4 inches.

Rim fire (.22's) are low powered cartridges. Someone on drugs may not feel the pain or be bothered much unless you hit a vital organ because the little bullets don't do a lot of damage. If all you have is a .22, keep on loading lead into your customer 'til the gun is empty. Otherwise, the perp can get back up—-with a temper. A .22 magnum, does more damage, but still not enough. Since you can't hand load a rim fire, you're stuck with the manufacturer's bullet. Penetration through a barricade or even heavy over clothes can be poor.

Center fire cartridges smaller than .38 Special are .25, and .32 or .380 (a mini 9 millimeter—-best of the small ones). Unless a .38 Special is too much gun for you, leave the smaller ones in the store.

The main consideration in purchasing a firearm is this: **Buy a gun you can handle.**

Don't exceed your limitations, but choose weapons that provide all the power you can manage, as well as all the weight you are able to carry comfortably. Remember, some specialty ammo adds effectiveness to your handgun. Good defense loads are available from Remington (Golden Saber) Federal (Hydra-shock) and Winchester (Black Talons).

If you want more firepower than a five or six shot .38 Special provides, go to 9 mm. The 9 mm. handguns can hold as many as 19 rounds; that's real fire power.

The .357 magnum shoots the same diameter bullet as the .38 Special—only faster. Make sure you can handle the weight, blast, and recoil before you invest, otherwise your pistol will stay at home. If you go for a 9 mm., ask your gun dealer to supply ammunition with stopping power. A wide variety is available.

The .41 magnum, in our opinion, is not a practical choice for a home defense weapon. The size, weight, high cost, and lack of choice in ammunition variety are the reasons for our decision.

The .44 magnum jumped in popularity when the gun jumped in *Dirty Harry's* hand. It was billed as the "most powerful handgun in the world." Audiences got a thrill when Harry told the bank robber, "Go ahead...make my day." The recoil of the weapon as filmed was only slightly exaggerated. It can smack you. Believe what you saw. Believe also the eardrum-busting muzzle blast. Maybe you should pass.

On the other hand, you may already own a .44 mag which you find difficult to shoot accurately. If that's the case, try .44 Special ammo. The reduced blast and recoil may be all you need to keep you on target accurately. These .44 Specials make an excellent choice for defense.

Finally, we discuss the famed .45 automatic. It normally pushes a 230 grain (heavy) projectile out the barrel at about 850 feet per second (relatively slow) which causes the bullet to stay in the target, as opposed to rush through and hit something behind the target. Of course, other weights are available, and lighter bullets travel faster. But the .45 pistol can be tough to shoot accurately unless you're prepared to spend plenty of time and money for practice ammo.

Huber says: "A compact revolver, chambered for a mid-powered cartridge is generally the best choice for a defense weapon." But his ten year old son consistently produces five shot groups under 5 inches from ten yards with Craig's work-weapon, a Custom Colt .45 auto with bells and whistles making it worth about $1,500. Dad and son practice a lot together.

You'll have a lot to learn with a .45 auto. The model 1911 and subsequent series (for the year they first came out) are still popular today and a lot of them are around, in homes, on firing ranges etc. Unlike more modern designs, they can fire without a magazine inserted, so the weapon is **not clear** just because you remove a full magazine. Also, holding your thumb up behind the slide while firing can cause severe pain and injury. If you're thinking of buying a .45, think again. Hitting a crook with a light bullet is far better than missing him with a heavy one. Make sure you can handle any big caliber before you buy. Remember, you can make a smaller caliber handgun much more effective with custom ammunition.

PLAN ON GETTING SHOT
People buy magazines and books all the time which teach them how to shoot. Those of us who watch TV and movies enjoy the fantasy of combat shooting. Also Nobody wants to read a book entitled, *HOW TO GET SHOT*.

Even so, we know that failing to prepare is the same as preparing to fail. The problem is this: Most people who buy guns fantasize about shooting someone else---but they seldom consider what it would be like the other way around. Nevertheless, we recommend you think that way. Why do you want to be first with a handgun? So you're not second. Think about getting shot. Thinking about being second in a gunfight is the best motivation to make you work hard so you'll always be first. Still, we live in a world where we often don't have the time or money to practice.

156

Therefore, we don't always practice shooting enough to become fast and accurate. If that's the case with you, consider ducking. Just because Marshall Dillon simply stood there is no reason for you not to run and shoot as you move.

Always try ~~to be the first one to shoot~~ never to be the second one to shoot. (Statement now politically correct) Dress for the occasion; wear a bullet proof (resistant) vest. Take cover. Cover and concealment are not the same. To conceal yourself means to hide---in bushes, in deep grass, or perhaps behind a grove of bamboo. Bullets can find you in those places, even though the shooter may not see you. For cover, get behind a big tree, a rock or a concrete block wall. If you can't take cover, drop down into the <u>smallest</u> mass your body will allow you to create. Baseball batters frequently crouch a little to cause pitchers to miss the zone. You'd be surprised at how small you can make your body while still being able to shoot as well as ever. Think of this: If you can compress or reduce your body mass to one third of its normal size, you reduce his target hitting ability by 66%! Finally, don't worry about it if you do get hit. Learn that getting shot does not mean you are going to die. The damage a pistol round does comes about because of a. physiological destruction, (tissue damage, nerve destruction or hemorrhage) and b. psychological destruction, such as mental breakdown due to panic, which causes psychogenic shock.

It's this latter, (b) problem that frequently causes death, and it doesn't have to happen. Many people who get shot keep on functioning long afterwards because they don't even know they were hit. So don't look down, see a new hole in your body, and then fall over. Your first lesson: It's better for you if you don't realize you're hit; but if you **do** become aware of the fact, shake it off. Second, we all have an abnormal fear of injury, pain, blood, or perhaps death, something akin to fear of snakes. But <u>fear</u> is what kills, not the stuff we're afraid of. Third, shooting wounds create a tremendous fear of the unknown because Hollywood always shows us the concocted worst. That isn't reality; don't be afraid. Countless people were shot in Vietnam (and for that matter, any big U.S. city) everyday. The vast percentage live---but that's why they don't make the news. Only the dead ones appear in print and the cause of death for many of them (I'll wager) was probably psychogenic shock, what I call the APD syndrome. (1. Awareness, 2. Prayer, 3. Death by conscious decision.) So it goes, 1. Ouch! 2. My God! 3. I think I have to die now.

Now, what about a., the damage a handgun bullet does to our bodies? In most cases, a wounding shot creates about the same trauma as a compound fracture. **It's entirely fixable.** Now, if you take a CNS (Central Nervous System) hit, you may die, <u>but you won't feel it anyway.</u> Otherwise, you can carry on, shoot back, and probably cause this confrontation to end in your favor. As soon as you can, do this: Stop the bleeding, (perhaps protect the wound) and treat for shock. Get medical help right away and you should recover.

SHOTGUNS
One well placed shot from any shotgun will terminate just about any home defense problem. Anybody who has seen the devastation a shotgun can do at close range has developed healthy respect for this weapon. The thought of a loaded shotgun in the hands of a homeowner causes criminals to have nightmares. If I were a burglar and heard the rack of a shell into a shotgun's chamber, I'd be gone!

Like handgun calibers, shotgun shells also come large and small—called gauges. This is tricky because the bigger the number, the smaller the gauge. The quick fix: Ladies get a 20 gauge with a three inch chamber, and most men can handle a 12 gauge. The other sizes don't make a whole lot of sense.

Once you've purchased the correct gauge, think about shot charge. At least it's consistent with gauges; the bigger the number, the smaller the shot. So #2 shot is bigger than #4, and #8 shot is a load commonly used for hunting small birds. For defense purposes, at ranges less than 20 feet, a load of #2's or #4's will do just fine. Don't buy steel shot for defense, especially in moist, tropical climates. Long storage periods in damp climates can cause the shot to rust together, which jeopardizes the shotgun when fired. To be ready for longer range shooting, (+50 yards) go to a double-ought buck load, (designated 00-BUCK on the box). In a plastic cup, you get 9 balls, each about a third of an inch in diameter, flying towards your target at 1050 feet per second. That's OK, but what I really like is the spread. Shotguns are also called scatter guns, and the farther away you are from a target, the wider the pattern. Of course, too far away and all the shot may land *around* the target, rather than *on* it. Also, you need to know: the smaller the shot, (bigger number) the less effective it will be at long range. That's why some of us prefer slugs for long range shooting.

What do you do if you can afford only one shotgun---a 12 gauge---and your wife is 5'-2" at 110 pounds? Visit your local skeet range. Almost every shooter reloads, and they can make you any shell you need. Cut the shot load down for your wife, and mix in dry oatmeal with the powder charge---until she's comfortable when she shoots.

You **must** pattern your shotgun. Otherwise, you'll never know where it shoots. Simply shoot carefully at a marked spot on a large cardboard box and see where all the shot goes. You're hoping for an evenly dispersed pattern around your aim point. If not, see a gunsmith.

Shotguns are smoothbore guns, so they get a slug to twist as it flies out of the barrel by putting vanes in the slug. Properly called rifled slugs, these reach out farther than shot loads, and provide enough accuracy to be effective up to 100 yards, where they shoot 8" groups.

If you read *Great Livin' in Grubby Times,* (found at most Army/Navy stores), you'll learn why a shotgun is a better choice for survival. They are cheaper and out-perform a pistol by quite a margin. For home defense, shotguns' big advantage is the noise they make---not when shot, but when racked. But, shotguns require two hands to shoot and can't be concealed easily. They're cumbersome in tight spaces. If you get a shotgun, folding stocks are a good idea, and laser sighting systems are wonderful for night work. Flashlights give away your position and draw fire. Also, the 12 gauge recoil often breaks flashlight bulbs.

Do you want an automatic, pump or double barrel? Doubles are fine because they are super reliable. Also, most home defense situations are decided with one shot, and your double gives you an extra shot (quick) for reinforcement. Like auto pistols, auto scatterguns become temperamental with no TLC. A light load in an auto shotgun may make it fail to feed. Also, all ammunition doesn't fit in all automatics. If you buy a box of shells which doesn't chamber correctly, the gun can't fire. Pumps require muscle but are more reliable. I vote for the pump. It will be as reliable as your racking arm. Don's was cheap; it's a S&W 3000 with folding stock. The tubular magazine under the barrel holds 7 rounds. He says, "Like an automatic pistol, this is a LIFO loader. Therefore, I put two slugs in first. (To chamber and fire last). In a close quarter battle, I'll never fire them. That's because tubular magazines on most shotguns provide you with a wonderful facility, you can reload anytime, anywhere, with zero down time (time when the weapon can't be fired). You just stuff shells into the tube, either while changing position or safe behind a barricade." On the other hand, Craig says, "If I could only have one weapon for home defense, I'd choose my Remington 870. It's smooth and reliable; I've owned mine for 25 years."

We leave rifles out of this discussion because they're a long range weapon. Criminals who want to rob and attack you do it from close range.

Finally, you need to understand something about weapons very few people consider, probably because of the way Hollywood portrays gunfights. There's a definite hierarchy of weapons, and to stay alive, you need to understand it---then respect it. Most people using handguns can't shoot as accurately or effectively at a long distance as they can with a shoulder-fired, long barreled weapon.

Handguns are most effective if you shoot at close range and shoot first. If you plan on using your .38 Special to tangle with a shotgun or rifle at long range (over 50 yards), buy life insurance. To survive in any shooting disagreement, this general rule applies:

Try to avoid combat with a weapon. Break off contact, give up your goods, or come back from a different angle with a new weapon. But don't risk your life if you have another option. No matter how good you are, remember this: You probably care about life; he never did. You don't get high on drugs; he is. You will get a paycheck next week and enjoy your life; his future is dismal.

**Therefore---on that fateful day, he won't hesitate;
you can't afford to hesitate either ...**

As part of that philosophy, never draw your weapon if you're not absolutely ready to shoot. Drawing a pistol in close (grappling range) quarters with your attacker could cause you to lose it. Witness the number of police officers shot with their own gun.

As long as you'll be packing iron around, get a concealed weapons permit for each adult. Call and ask what the requirements are before you appear in person.

Many jurisdictions require that you state you were raped or you carry payroll money and feel at risk before they'll issue. To get a permit, you have to tell them what they want to hear.

Finally, stay in good physical condition. You'd be surprised at how your muscles deteriorate without exercise. Criminals are looking for weak victims, and you will look weak if you let yourself get out of shape. Aerobic exercise three times a week is best. Add some gym training for muscle tone. If you spend the time to stay in shape, you'll look alert. Having an effective weapon on your person with which you are competent will also give you a confident attitude. Most criminals read that attitude as a "detour-to-some-other-victim" sign.

With regular shooting practice and a constant awareness of your surroundings, your quick access to firepower will make your chances of winding up in the news as a victim substantially less.

GANGS, GUNS AND PROPERTY?

Ownership of anything is determined by who has dominion and control over it. You don't own property because it's registered in your name or because you pay the taxes on it. You don't own it if anyone can take it from you without restraining force or fear of punishment. Maybe the real owner of your property is the neighborhood gang.

"Who joins a gang?" I asked. A sheriff's gang specialist answered, "Everybody. If a kid doesn't join, then every day, they beat him up, steal his lunch money, and make his life miserable until he joins. Once they join, they never quit. Today, the oldest East L.A. gang member is 63 years old, and still has respect and power."

Some politicians think gun control in the U.S. is the answer to crime, which has increased 560% since early 1960. Hardened criminals and gangbangers want more gun control. Even if they get caught with a gun after killing someone, they are seldom charged with the possession because a capital crime overrides less serious charges. But good citizens go unarmed and obey the law, which makes them easy targets, and a criminal's life delightful.

We deliberately left basic shooting instruction out of this book because beginners' firearms instruction must be learned in the hands-on mode. Take a course. Here, we teach things you might not learn in basic study.

Chapter 11

ADVANCED FIREARMS TRAINING

As a beginner, you can't learn how to shoot well from a book or video. You really need hands-on training. Call the National Rifle Association and find out where classes are held. You have so many things to learn in the beginning that you can't concentrate on all of it. Instructors help make sure you stay safe; also a trained shooter watches as you actually shoot, analyzes your shot groups, and corrects any errors you make either when shooting or loading.

You must learn the basics of firearms marksmanship before you can start to develop defensive shooting capabilities. In basics, for example, you learn how the weapon works, how to align the sights, and how to make those *aligned* sights stay on

SIGHTS PERFECTLY ALIGNED

| White Dots for night | Regular notch 'n post |

target. Examples of defensive combat shooting techniques are speed reloading, speed drawing, and shooting from behind barricades. Trying any of these before you learn the basics could be dangerous.

Shooting a handgun well requires constant practice. You can't miss and finish second in a field of two. In a high percentage of encounters with a criminal, one shot settles the question of who keeps on breathing. Therefore, you have to be smooth and effective with your first round. Even if you can't get to the range, dry fire at the guys on your TV screen. Just watch your sights. Learn to focus on the front sight so that the things you shoot at appear as a blur.

Most people practice by going to a range and calmly firing at paper targets. The ranges are open from 9:00 A.M. to 5:00 P.M. They practice diligently and use ear protection. The LAPD (PD=Police Dept). recommends shooting 1,000 rounds a year. Do that. You can make a hobby out of it and win trophies. But take note of this if you do what most do: <u>You'll shoot during the daylight hours—-outdoors.</u>

After all this, you'll think you're ready. You and your handgun have become good friends and you understand each other. Have you noticed this, however? One good crime deterrent is night lighting. Why? Because most criminals have a neurosis about being in light. Guess what? You may be as good as the Lone Ranger in daylight outdoors with your Mickey-Mouse ears on, but your most likely criminal encounter will take place in the dark indoors where gun fire is explosive. You'll not only be exposed to your own muzzle flashes, but perhaps to someone else's.

Of course you're scared. It's dark. You can't see your sights. The muzzle flash of a pistol in the dark will scare you severely, and if you look at it, your night vision will disappear, perhaps causing you to panic because it appears you went blind at a critical moment. The indoor bang will jar you out of your wits.

Now, given this drastic change in shooting conditions, change the way you practice. **Learn how to shoot at**

night. You have to shoot indoors a couple of times without hearing protection. Learn not to look directly at your muzzle flash. Nighttime aiming techniques are different. The distance between you and your target will probably be much less than you ever thought about.

Of course, you have to develop speed. When bullets are flying around, he who hesitates quits breathing shortly thereafter. Many people think of the speed concept as being fast on the draw. That's not true. It's being first on the draw. As soon as you even get a whiff of possible trouble, your hand should be in your bag, under your coat, or behind your back getting control of your weapon. If you draw the weapon completely, perhaps use a rag, towel, or folded newspaper to cover it so it's ready to shoot when you make a decision.

Ready. Now, watch and listen carefully. If the trouble really develops, ~~shoot first~~ don't shoot second. Don't consider yourself to be the Lone Ranger. It isn't that you want to develop the mental resolve to be a killer; you **do** want to develop the mental resolve <u>not to be a victim</u>.

If you decide to shoot, <u>timing and accuracy</u> go hand and hand. It won't do you one tiny bit of good to fire fast and miss. Never shoot so fast that you only punch holes in the air. That kind of thing happens when you haven't practiced, feel less confident, and are faced with the enormity of a life-death situation. That's why we teach you how to get shot <u>at</u>. If you don't think you can shoot first to solve the problem, take cover immediately; then perhaps duke it out from a place where you know the likelihood of your getting hit is minimal.

> "I determined the maximum practical range for my own home defense practice by measuring the longest distance I can see, point to point, in my own home. Sixty six feet. I then added ten feet to this range. A little over 25 yards. I practice at ranges from five feet out to my maximum. I've resolved not to let a potential threat get closer than five feet as this could neutralize my ability to react."   *Craig*

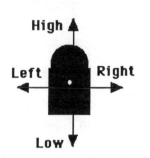

ONLY FOUR WAYS YOU CAN MISS

High

Left   Right

Low

The purpose of shooting at a target is to hit. That's the opposite of miss. To hit your target, learn how <u>not</u> to miss. Misses break down into two categories: You either miss off to one side (right/left) or you miss high/low. All you have to do is correct and eliminate the misses and every shot you fire will be a hit.

First, let's deal with left/right. Any good pistol shooter knows the method employed for marksmanship. Part of that is: *Align the sights (barrel) with the target, and then squeeze the trigger slowly so that you don't cause the barrel to mis-align.* Think of it this way: it's like taking a picture. Just as you can't move the camera when you shoot, you can't move the weapon when you fire. Assuming that you modified your barrel with Tulip paste, you have a straight phosphorescent line you can point at your target. After that, all you have to do is make sure not to move the weapon left or right when you squeeze the trigger.

Eliminate high and low misses by holding the barrel level. It takes practice. I've seen gunfights won by a fast first shot which hit the ground and sprayed pieces of asphalt and bullet fragments all over the adversary's lower body. Those mini-hits distracted him considerably, and bought time for a well-aimed second shot which won the contest, hands down. Naturally, you need a hard surface under you to make this work. But a round on the ground marks the shot so you can check for left right accuracy, **and** insures that your barrel is in line with the target. For this reason, I prefer to shoot low. Most handgun shooters tend to point high, especially from the hip. Then, they're confused because they don't know how they missed. Thus, they can't adjust aim on a second round.

Whenever you practice, <u>count shots forwards</u>. Continue to count under your breath; when the word "six" (if you shoot a six-shooter) comes up, you'd better reload. Counting also helps you to train yourself to know at all times how much ammo you've expended. When you get to heaven, you're going to meet people who got there early in life because they forgot to count. This is a critical skill and discipline in any weapons training. During a hot bullet exchange, you're highly at risk as soon as your weapon goes "down" that is---empties. To stay alive, you need to minimize down time. The key to reloading quickly isn't how fast you can do it, or what fancy gadgets you use. The key to speedy reloading is preparation, and you get ready with your loading hand on time when you count shots. Otherwise, you shoot and come up empty as a rather unpleasant surprise.

Here's something else critical to know: **Don't develop the bad habit of reloading only after your weapon empties. Reload when you have an opportunity, when your enemy least expects it, or any time you get the urge!** Overcome your lack of training in this area. At the range, during the day, with a range master in charge, you'll empty your pistol, then reload. But that has nothing to do with combat, and it's a dangerous habit to develop. Most handgun shooters do the same thing everywhere---fire until the weapon is empty---and then reload. Any criminal worth his stolen salt will be counting your shots and take advantage of your down time (weapon not loaded). In a prolonged gunfight, firing 'til empty could get you killed. Also, (especially for all the police officers who read this) learn to fire along with your partner so you reload at different times. Thus, you keep the advantage.

In defense, don't just think about shooting. Think also about getting shot <u>at</u>. The police think about it; that's why so many wear vests. Who might be shooting at you? Will they be any good? When I read H. Norman Schwartzkopf's, *It*

SHOOTING CONFRONTATION

FAST   SLOW

Doesn't Take a Hero, I learned how he conducted training---to win over the best. That's what you have to do as well. Consider that the criminal you go up against is cunning, street wise, battle-hardened, and ruthless. Let me tell you something about those kinds of guys; they often identify the weapon shooting at them and count shots. It's a good idea; almost everybody shoots and reloads in the Mother Goose mode---Empty-Dumpty. Not you, though. You want to pray that the guy against you is counting, then eject and load again after three. Fire three more and aim the fourth carefully. If he counts---he'll look---just about the time you enter your fourth round into the fire fight.

Of course, you count, both his and yours. Counting forward is also advantageous for mix 'n match shooters who need to know which round is up. For you, that's important because we want you to practice a lot with inexpensive ammo that will duplicate the recoil and velocity of your fighting loads. For the real thing, load out of several packages. Each round has a specific purpose. Two might be expanding shot shells. At long distances, or where

---

Note here that Craig disagrees with the concept of Mix 'n match loading. He prefers shooting ammo from a major manufacturer and settles on one load which performs well in his chosen weapon, with sufficient power and accuracy to get the job done.

You may feel the same. Reliability is the key; you simply cannot afford a malfunction. So even if you go for mix 'n match, use similar velocity cartridges and practice enough so you are absolutely sure your mix works in your weapon and performs on target without causing you to miss.

---

penetration is required, you'll need a Cor-Bon™, round, so shoot the other rounds you don't need now to perform that specific task. We call it, "shooting through." It's quicker and safer than trying to manipulate the cylinder by hand.

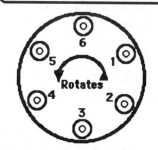

FIRING ORDER FOR MY RUGER SIX SHOT

With any handgun, mix 'n match every magazine or cylinder full of ammo the same. Thus, you can count forward and know exactly what round does what job of penetration, expansion, or long-distance placement. Say you want to shoot a custom bullet on the

Load with 1 Expanding shot; 2, a hollow point. Thumb past 3. Then shoot 4, a .357 magnum blaster to penetrate a barricade.

fourth shot. Auto magazines are simple to set up; they are LIFO loaders, (Last In, First Out) so you load three more after your custom round. Revolvers can be easy too; you set up the speed loader in the order you would like. But then---you have to match the speed loader to the revolver's cylinder. So you mark them both and line the marks up.

Use tulip paste on your cylinder at number five, and mark you speed loader the same way. Even in the dark, matching your speed loader to your cylinder will give you precisely the same mix of ammo.

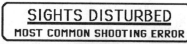

SIGHTS DISTURBED
MOST COMMON SHOOTING ERROR

Pulls shots down here.

The key to straight shooting is to acquire your target in the background of aligned sights, and then cause the hammer to fall without disturbing that sight alignment. You **can not learn** to be a good shot by reading a book. **You need** hands-on training.

DRY FIRING

You need to educate your trigger finger. To train it, load your revolver with spent shells (dead primer, no powder or bullet). Cock the hammer and watch the sights carefully as you squeeze the trigger. Your trigger finger disturbed the sight alignment if the sights move just as the hammer falls. When you can squeeze the trigger without disturbing the sight alignment, even in the least, you're ready to begin firing live ammo.

Have a friend load three rounds in your revolver and hand you the weapon, (hammer down) so you don't know when those rounds will fire. Shoot six. Three times the hammer will fall on an empty chamber, which is your opportunity to train yourself to watch your sights carefully as the hammer falls. The other three rounds should surprise you when they go off. Since you're now watching the sights as the gun fires, you should be able to call where the bullet will land. If the hole in the target is right where you think it should've been, then your trigger control has improved. But if you call the shot to land in one place and find a hole elsewhere, your trigger finger is shoving the barrel off just as the weapon fires. Work some more on dry firing. When you get control of your trigger, change your practice. Shoot at night, and shoot at body-sized targets, not bull's-eyes.

We push two kinds of training—-mental and physical—-with equal enthusiasm. Mechanical skills alone are not enough. Having the mental make-up to use those skills in combat is much more important. You **must** also train your mind to react promptly and forcibly to counter a violent threat.

FELONS. NO MORE ACCESS TO PUBLIC LANDS

If a judge can issue a restraining order to avoid a potential problem, why not restrict felons from certain public lands as well as private property owned by others? The idea is to make trespass by a convict a crime and therefore give citizens freedom to take a walk in a public park without fear. How to enforce? ID checks by patrol with NCIC computer reports over the radio.

Chapter 12

AFTER THE ATTACK

OUR LEGAL SYSTEM, A QUICK OVERVIEW

Criminal law is different than civil law, both in procedure and in what's allowable as evidence. The state brings charges through a prosecutor against suspects or alleged criminals who are considered innocent until proved guilty. Minor crimes are misdemeanors; major crimes are felonies, which in most localities are divided into Class A (most serious), B, and C felonies.

Whether you are a victim or you've been charged as a perpetrator, you'll be dealing with the State in criminal law. If you wound someone in self-defense or in defense of your home and property, you may also be dealing with him personally if he sues you in civil court for monetary damages. It often happens. The same person who considered your home his personal plundering ground will be aided by an attorney who considers 40% of anything collected to be your loss and his gain. Therefore, wounding a perpetrator is a bad idea. If you must shoot, don't wound. More important, don't hesitate, which is something you might do because of your uncertainty about our laws. Trying to be right in the eyes of the law has caused many innocent deaths. It's much better if you strive to be righteous.

You want to be right. <u>Much more important, you need to think you're right.</u> If you're not sure, then you'll come into conflict with an enemy germ who will act as if they are sure (because they've already chosen not to care) and they'll shoot faster and attack more ferociously because they're more committed to battle. That's often why victims lose.

So get right. After the dust settles and the blood spills, the best way to do that is to apply the same principles we've laid with regard to crime generally. Your *after* depends on what you do *before.*

IF YOU WON
Be it on the street, in your home, your vehicle, or anywhere else, you came out victorious. You may not have won unscathed but you've survived. Now how do you survive the aftermath? The guilt....the possible legal problems....the natural curiosity of your friends, neighbors and family.....the unwanted publicity.....?

Your basic problem, if authorities examine the evidence, is to show that your life was in danger. If you were faced with a knife or other deadly weapon, your fear was certainly justified. Therefore, your actions will be likewise justified. It doesn't matter where the knife came from. Even if it was part of a matched set out of your very own kitchen, the fact that the perp had it in his hand (his fingerprints on the handle) will help. Your testimony (after being counseled by an attorney) that he was threatening you will also help.

<u>Be advised</u>: Don't tamper with evidence! Even if you think what you are doing may enhance your case for self defense, you may, in fact, destroy valuable evidence that would have made the case for you. Forensic science is one area of the law which has improved tremendously. Some of the best police work in the country is now done in

laboratories. I've heard statements by people who want to defend their homes and are half paranoid due to the high crime rate. They say, "Heck, if he comes up to my window, I'll blow him away, then drag him inside."

Sorry. That <u>won't</u> work! Any hunter knows you can't move a bleeding animal without leaving a blood trail a blind man could follow. Even without a blood trail, footprints outside your house will reveal just how the event took place. On the other hand, if the person lying on the ground outside your house also had a gun lying there with his prints on it, it's more logical to believe you were afraid he would shoot at you through the window if you didn't shoot first.

"What is it with clients? Why don't they call me and ask, 'What will happen if I slit my throat?' Instead, they call me and ask, 'I just slit my throat. What's next?'" S. D. Atty Nelson Millsberg

No matter what the circumstances were that lead you to shoot, first call your attorney. He is an officer of the court. After you've explained to your attorney what happened and been counseled, then your attorney can surrender you to proper authorities and stay there with you for questioning. This is important.

CONSIDER LEGAL PROBLEMS
Before committing mentally to shoot in self defense, it's a good idea to contact the Attorney General in your state and ask for copies of laws pertaining to self defense.

Contact an attorney, many of whom specialize. Many law firms hire at least one criminal specialist, usually someone with prosecutorial experience. Hiring a real estate attorney to advise you about criminal law is like hiring a podiatrist to do brain surgery. Initial consultations are inexpensive; call and talk to any attorney's secretary, who will probably quote around $25. Some attorneys charge more. Ask friends for recommendations.

Then visit the attorney. Perhaps take him to lunch at a restaurant. This is a crucial part of your defense planning. Since most crime occurs after hours, will your attorney take a call at home? Is there a special number? Will he take a call and respond immediately if ever needed? Can you surrender to her or him and let them decide what to tell the police, including whether or not you were the person who did the shooting? Discuss billing.

Since all of your conversations with your attorney are private and privileged, nothing you say to your attorney can ever be used against you. If you make a mistake and shoot too fast, your attorney's job is to see that you get the best possible defense. As a matter of professional pride, your attorney does not want to see you go to jail.

AT THE TIME OF THE INCIDENT
If you haven't called the police prior to the battle, and you won, don't call now. Call your criminal attorney. Follow his or her advice. You don't have to answer any questions from anyone. Direct all inquiries to your attorney.

Never take a chance on your police, prosecutor, or the courts. They may be—-no, they are—-often the nicest people in your community. But if you share information, thoughts, or even your grocery bill with one of them after you're charged with a crime, they will use that information against you if it will help convict. It's not personal. That's their job. **If you're arrested but not Mirandized, (had your rights read to you) speak no further with the police and tell your attorney immediately.** Many crooks and thieves, have foiled police; others have been released on technicalities. Authorities always need a higher percentage of convictions. Thus, police and prosecutors will use anything you say against you. When they warn you, **they are not kidding.**

If you get a Miranda warning ("You have a right to remain silent. . ."), do just that! Talk to nobody. You'll have this uncontrollable urge to explain. You'll feel a need to make others think you were right. **Don't!** One nice way to stop them from asking further questions is to say: "Thank you, gentlemen. This interview is terminated as of now."

Likewise, never grant interviews to the press. Press coverage does very little good for you. Other criminals may want to try to find out firsthand what was worth dying for. If they can successfully rip off something their former dead associate could not, so much the better for them. Fellow gang members of the deceased might consider vengeance to honor their jacket colors. You <u>are required</u> to stay at the scene of an accident. (Even that is changing, however; you may now drive away slowly if you suspect the shady looking characters behind you and you think you were bumped on purpose. You are <u>not required</u> to stay at the scene of a crime. In many situations, I would leave immediately. For example, if I were riding my bike or horse on a lonely stretch of road and I was suddenly accosted and I shot the suspect I would leave. Real reason: I don't trust the system. Stated reason: Fear. Most perpetrators in remote places operate in pairs or gangs, and they wouldn't rely on the system either.

CAN YOU TRUST THE POLICE TO BE ON YOUR SIDE?
In recent New York Police Commissioner hearings, the witness, a former cop now in jail, said, ". . .We would take drugs, rob, steal, lie on police reports, and beat citizens with flashlights and sticks any time we wanted. We used to go into brothels, yank the johns out of bed, and force the hooker to have sex with us. They were terrified, so we settled them down by saying, 'It's OK, we're cops.'" *Reported in USA Today, Oct 93. Serpico,* back from exile in Europe, commented, "Corruption goes clear to the top."

The best response you can give to the idle curious is to say nothing at all. If you must speak, say, " I wish it hadn't happened, I had no other choice, my life was at stake." **That's all.** No philosophy, no condemnation of the system and no verbal attack on the deceased. Never express guilty feelings or remorse about the act of taking another's life, not even to your closest friends. Your feelings of guilt or remorse might be construed to indicate you had a choice. Your position should always be:

    1. You were faced with a set of circumstances which left you no alternative.

    2. You were in mortal fear for your life and in fear for the lives of loved ones at the time of the incident.

GUILT

Even though you had no other choice and you were 100% right to kill in self defense, you may experience guilt feelings over taking another human life. Homicide is an ominous word. The prohibition against killing is so deeply ingrained in most of us that the phrase, "justifiable homicide" can cause subconscious feelings of guilt.

Here's the cure: Think realistically about what happened. In all probability, you didn't take one life; you saved several. Most violent criminals are never rehabilitated. They go on destroying lives as long as they live.

Reflect on the alternatives. How much more guilt would you feel if you didn't act positively and, as a result, some member of your family ended up badly injured or dead? The guilt over killing some felon who is threatening your life will go away. The guilt over the death of a loved one will probably last forever.

**The best way to lengthen an innocent life---
is to shorten a criminal's.**   *Don*

VICTIM'S GUILT

If you're a victim of a crime involving breach of common morality or perversion, you may feel shame and degradation. That's what we've encountered with child victims of rape. Older, more clever perpetrators always manage to make the victim feel guilty because "they took part in a terrible thing." In phone counseling, their first job is often to convince the caller that she is, in fact, a victim, rather than a co-perpetrator. Why? If someone (stepfather, uncle, or boyfriend) rapes a child and convinces her or him it was their fault, they don't tell---often for years.

Also, consider this. For years, police thinking on the subject of rape was this: You don't die if you submit. Therefore, many victims submitted. Now, however, we've learned: Post-submission guilt trauma is psychological death. Submission helped cause an increase in that crime rate. You can beat 60% of rapists if you put up a fight.

IF YOU LOST

If you've been the victim of a violent crime, knowing your attackers were caught and have a high probability of punishment is somewhat comforting. So you want to do your best to make that happen. If you lost and survived, learn from your own experience.

As the victim or witness, you can do certain things to help insure criminals will be caught and brought to justice. By doing that, you help healing, both physical and mental. You also send a message to other would-be attackers: "Crime can be risky business."

This is what to do:

1. Report the attack as soon as possible. No matter how embarrassing the circumstances, report everything to the authorities. No information in connection with an attack is too unimportant to report. The smallest detail may lead to the first break in a case. Give detailed and specific

descriptions of the attackers. Describe or show the area where the attack took place, and describe any potential witness you saw around the crime scene as well. Describe all the vehicles you saw in the area. Any cats or dogs in the area at the time of attack should be noted, too; the pet's owner may have been a witness. Maybe the kid who owns the bike that was leaned against a tree witnessed what happened, so take note if a bike was there. Make sure the time of the attack, beginning to end, is noted accurately.

2. Preserve physical evidence. Don't sweep up broken glass at the entry site. Don't put chairs or tables upright and back in place. Don't touch anything that may have been touched by the assailant(s). When the attack involves body contact with an attacker, don't change clothes, bathe, wash, or comb your hair. Lots of evidence can be found on the victim's body after a struggle.

3. Let any news release come from the police or the prosecutor's office. Don't discuss the attack on the telephone unless you know you're talking with an officer involved in the case. Never discuss the attack with an attorney who represents the criminals unless directed to do so by the prosecutor. In crimes committed by someone the victim knows personally, attorneys for the accused attacker, thief, or rapist have been known to threaten the victim with defamation or another crime in order to secure the release of their client.

Example: Rape case in the victim's home; husband present. After the crime, the rapist was subdued and captured. Prior to the perp's trial, his attorney threatened the victim-wife with exposure to husband for having carried on previous affair with rapist. Even though her marriage and reputation was threatened, she didn't drop charges. The truth: The rapist was a complete stranger.

4. Prepare to testify in the event of a trial. Write down every detail of what happened as soon as you can. In the cases where you were the victim of a vicious or morally reprehensible crime, a natural part of healing is memory loss of the sordid details. Several months later, a defense attorney for the accused will probably use that memory loss and cleverly cross examine you in an attempt to prove your testimony unreliable.

DO ALL THE *BEFORE* THINGS PRIOR TO THE *AFTER*

Hopefully you will never have to defend yourself or your family against an attack. If you've followed the advice in earlier chapters, you'll see how much trouble it has been to avoid. Transcience alarms, Maxwell screens, Sabre Gas--- all of it keeps you from having to suffer a criminal encounter. If somehow they get to you anyway, though, you and your family will have a far better chance of surviving if you're prepared.

When all the *before* things are accomplished, your *after* will be a lot easier.

DESIGNATED CARRIERS

In high crime areas, concealed weapons permits are almost impossible to obtain. Witness L.A., where the designated chief of police couldn't obtain a permit. As it stands now, the nation's capital of crime, Washington, D.C. issues no weapons permits to anyone (including retired FBI) other than local (D.C.) police retired---which leaves the area wide open for criminals.

The Federal government is missing a great opportunity to make use of all kinds of people whom they could license to carry anywhere. Retired police officers, federal and state, retired military officers, and several other catagories of responsible individuals, one of whom might have decided to ride a subway in New York, and thus saved many lives during the shooting massacre of late '93.

WHY ARE CCW PERMITS SO HARD TO OBTAIN?

City and country governments don't want to issue because of liability. If the do issue and the citizen with a permit makes a shooting mistake, some attorneys have named the issuing government as co-defendants (deep pockets) and therefore liable. Thus, the only citizens who can carry are street thugs, for whom the local government is not liable. Or, are they? (Nobody admits to having created the mess.)

GOING INTO WAR AT A DISADVANTAGE

When the average law-abiding citizen and the criminal come into conflict, the outcome of the conflict will be dictated by the experience, will to fight, weaponry and skill of the two combatants.

As a law-abiding citizen, you stand to lose in all three areas. Criminals have more skill because they have more experience in street fighting. With welfare to take care of their needs, they have plenty of time to plan and practice. Citizens have less fighting skill because they have jobs and therefore less time to practice defense measures. Criminals have better weaponry because they don't care about laws controlling guns, which citizens obey. Criminals have a tremendous will to fight because they feel no restraint from criminal justice and are often reinforced by drugs. Law-abiders, on the other hand, don't really want to hurt anybody, and are afraid of arrest. They take no drugs to make themselves vicious. Winning could be worse than losing if the justice system later decides the intended victim committed a crime while fighting for survival.

Because of these differences in combatants, new laws must give defending citizens a special legal status, and presuppose that victim-defenders operate with a restricted or diminished mental capacity. This presupposition would give winning victims a benefit in trial, as well as relief from civil liability after a shooting.

SECURE FROM CRIME
Box Additions Index

Box Additions are inserted in the text to give the reader's mind a pause and refresh concentration on the main topic.

Topical Index

a

SECURE FROM CRIME

Glossary

AUTOMATIC PISTOL. Really, semi-auto, which means you have to squeeze the trigger each time you wan the weapon to fire, but that a new cartridge will automatically feed into the chamber. The other kind of handgun: revolver.

BAGGIE. Usually zip-lock, to hide auto registrations in trunk, and guns under sand.

BULLET. What comes out of a cartridge case through the barrel when fired.

CARTRIDGE. Case, plus primer & powder to propel bullet through barrel on a firearm.

CASE. To inspect and investigate potential theft or burglary victim.

DefCon. Short for Defense Condition, it's a new system to help you confront danger before it becomes a severe problem.

ENERGY. Amount of force conveyed to target by projectile.

FIREPOWER. Here, not so much what heavy bullets comes out of the muzzle or how fast they fly, but, how many rounds the handgun holds.

GERM In this book, a human who infects society by preying on victims.

INDEX. The way your handgun fits in your shooting hand (should never change). Hold fingers and thumb in a "V." Keep barrel in line with forearm.

LAG TIME Fatal to armed victims---it's the hesitation to act because of fear of prison, etc.

MACE. Common variety of tear gas spray. New versions add pepper and blind the perp.

Mr COLT. Name of early American firearms inventor.

NCIC National Criminal Information Center

PD Police Department. Normally preceded by other letters, such as M, for Miami PD.

PERP. Short for perpetrator---one who commits crime. Commonly used by police.

PRESENTATION. The act of removing your handgun from it's storage place (shoulder, ankle, or belt holster, or fanny pack) and acquiring a target.

RUGER. Master designer of super-quality firearms known all over for reliability.

SANCTUARY. Safe room in your house. Name came first from use of church to secure fugitives from persecution.

SMITH & WESSON. Old and popular American Firearms makers mostly handguns.

SNUFF. Real murder of a woman or child in a pornographic movie to increase voyeurs' thrill.

TARGET ACQUISITION. You acquire a target when the sights are properly aligned and the target shows up as a blur just over the front blade.

DISCOUNT COUPON

Tear out this page or copy it on a Xerox. Use this discount coupon to order any of our books on the other side of this page.

Path Finder Books are guaranteed. If your book suffers water damage, fire, or consumption by goat, we'll send a new one for half price.

When ordering, add $1.35 for shipping and handling after deducting the discount amount on the coupon to the left.

Dealers and book stores: Please accept this coupon on any of Path Finder's books. We guarantee to redeem this for you in keystone product.

Path Finder Publications
1296 E. Gibson Rd, E-301
Woodland, Ca. 95776